If ONLY Someone Had Told Me

Wickedly Straight Talk About Parenting Kids Ages 0-6

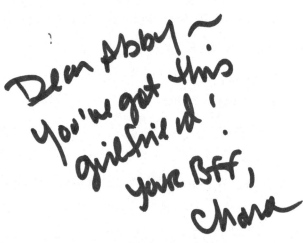

Dear Abby ~
You've got this
girlfriend!
Your BFF,
Chara

Chara Burnett & Helen Waters

If ONLY Someone Had Told Me

ISBN: 978-0-692-45641-5

First Edition – April 2015

Dedicated to our husbands Crick & Keith, and children Wyatt, Alexandra, Skylar & Carter

Encouragers:
Richard Alexander, Ariel Balter, Paige Cattano, Byung Choung, Dane Christensen, Markus Covert, Lucy Dathan, Vanessa Davies, Robbie Fang, Tom Hayse, Rob Henderson, Simona Jankowski, Nandini Joseph, Annamaria Konya, Gillian MacKenzie, Liz Maguire, Lara McDonald, Elaine Orr, Cathleen Pearson, David Peery, RS, Joy Peacock, Kara Reiter, Adelaide Roberts, Jennifer Titus, Ang, Rachel Thomas, MPJ and Wedge Martin.

Contributors:
Holly Abrams, Editor
Adrienne Defendi, Photo Copyright
Ashlie Benton, Cover Image Copyright
Matt Gilman, Web Design

Please spread the word about our indie-parenting book: from two moms to other moms – a BFF guide!

* Tell your friends!
* Review Us On Amazon.com
* Like Us On Facebook: If Only Someone Had Told Me
* Follow Us On Twitter @badassmoms

Table of Contents

Introduction

How This Book Came To Be

Before we went into our respective labors, we hadn't spent a lot of time around very young children or their parents, but we sure had read a lot of books about babies and child rearing. Then we gave birth... and started to face facts.

As if overnight, our lives seemed filled with ridiculous difficulties – expensive, competitive, time-consuming and fear-driven. Where was the simple, loving life that had been touted in articles about Quality Bonding With Baby? Toddling With Your Toddler? Like waiting for a punch line that never came, our sense of *holy-crap-this-can't-be-happening* didn't diminish as the kids got a bit older... it compounded. Somehow, all those helpful books – *What to Expect When You're Expecting*, *The Girlfriend's Guide to Pregnancy*, even *I Don't Know How She Does It* – did not scratch the surface when it came to preparing us appropriately for being a parent with children under the age of seven.

Helen:

My husband comes from a swimming family, and he swam in college. He swims on a master's team that includes a couple of Olympians. I am a good athlete and a solid swimmer. With that, I assumed our kids would learn to swim and enjoy it – in pools, lakes, oceans, the whole nine yards. They'd take lessons, they'd practice the strokes, and bada-bing-bada-boom, done. Fast forward to 2003, with our first child. It's summertime, and he's five or six months old: chubby, diapered, drinking lots of formula, maybe starting on a bit of rice cereal, and not yet sleeping through the night. (Oy!)

One day I came home from a group playdate in a lather. The other parents had been comparing swim schools for their six-month-old babies. One school in particular seemed to be all the rage. Apparently it was "absolutely the BEST," had the world's longest waitlist, and therefore you had to "take whatever is available, like Thursdays at 11:15 am." And get this – the other babies in my playgroup were already registered in Baby and Me swimming classes for $90 per month! That's essentially a half-hour, $20 playdate at the pool each week. Meanwhile, I'm thinking, "Don't swim lessons start when you're four or five years old … at the YMCA? What IS a Baby and Me class – is it like Wild Kingdom, where parents throw babies in the water to see which ones start paddling? How did you guys hear out about 'the BEST swim school' in the first place? Am I the only one whose baby isn't registered? I don't think I can leave work every Thursday for a baby swim lesson, since it's a one-hour commute each way. Oh my god. Oh my god." And I swear, among the families we knew, my kids were the only ones who did not attend this swim school. For years, every time swimming came up, I changed the subject!"

Chara:
When you hear the term 'acid reflux', what comes to mind? Maybe you imagine a health condition that strikes middle-aged overeaters, treated by remedies with names like 'the Purple Pill' or Zantac. Well guess what – my not-middle-aged, not-overeating baby had acid reflux AND IT MADE HER ACT LIKE A MONSTER. It never dawned on me that there could be a baby on Planet Earth who wouldn't happily suck on a pacifier OR drink from a baby bottle OR sit untroubled in a stroller or car seat OR be happy lying down. Thanks, acid reflux! As a new mom, I found myself racing home from work to feed her every 2½ hours, holding her upright over my shoulder 24/7 until I developed chronic upper body pain, nursing her to the point where I developed carpal tunnel syndrome, and dealing with her constant CONSTANT, crying. Wow. This wasn't the retirement

living I envisioned as a part-time Stay At Home Parent (SAHP). What happened to my dream of mothering a contented baby, sometimes awake and sometimes sleeping, while I filled in the quiet hours of the day with a bit of freelance work? Instead, I had become a crazed OCD woman, running red lights between feedings and threatening anyone who woke my rarely-sleeping, reflux-suffering child with acute bodily harm.

Your friends with kids must have known these things, right? Maybe they didn't speak up because they assumed you wouldn't willingly relate to this degree of ludicrousness. Perhaps they glossed over innumerable present-day screwed-up parenting realities by rationalizing, "it's just the way things are" – like a Kardashian racking up just another headline in People. Well, that didn't sit very well with us.

We wrote this book to help you deal with what's coming to a theater near you, instead of getting run over as a parent of a child under seven. We're talking out loud about the unmentionable, the unbelievable – the things that are too embarrassing to admit. We are sharing our perspectives on the hot mess in which we, and maybe you, are living.

Why Hasn't This Book Already Been Written?
Simple. It's way too un-PC to write this stuff.

FAQ

Is this book a rant?
Well… we do love to rant. But this book was actually our way of talking openly about many painful things that nobody owns up to, yet become part of life once you enter parenthood.

Are parents supposed to feel validated by these disclosures?
Yes. Otherwise, we just wasted 3 years of our lives writing this stupid book.

Do you assume everyone feels this way about parenting?
Of course not. But for those who do, reading this book should be quite a pick-me-up!

Do you regret having your own kids?
Not most days. But if we had had a book like this to prepare us, we would have been better off.

Are you telling people not to have kids?
Nope, that's none of our business. Why, are you rethinking it? Our intent is to simply unveil some major, mostly unspoken, hard realities of being a parent with kids under the age of seven.

Why did you write this book?
We wrote this book as a BFF guide – from two moms to other moms – about things you only discuss with your closest friends. Like writing a break-up/ love song, writing this book got the big gripes off our chests, providing an honest look at certain aspects of parenthood, enriched with practical advice.

Chapter 1

Your Vision of Parenting – #onebighallucination

A new parent's vision of parenthood is often comprised of romanti-cized, imaginative elements crafted by astute media minds. Popular child-rearing culture is devoted to spin, leading us to believe in fairy-dust fictional qualities that don't hold up in the harsh light of day. These go well beyond the power of positive thinking, and **once upon a time, it was called "tripping".**

Parenting is a significant, lifelong sacrifice. Yeah, sure … you've heard this so many times, but it doesn't truly sink in until it's your reality. People don't talk upfront about how hard it is to be a parent of children ages 0-6. Every new parent we've spoken with, whose kids are under age seven, agrees that parenting is far bigger and badder than they ever imagined. It can be tiring, tedious and feel like the payoff isn't coming for decades. Society keeps raising the bar on your obligations, too: unrelenting 'stan-dards' requiring blisteringly long hours, and continually putting someone else's needs before yours.

However, it is the height of un-PC to say any of this out loud, so we're putting it in print for you.

Helen:

I have to confess that I didn't give 'how to parent' any real thought, except to vow that I wouldn't be like my Tiger Mom and Dad, or any of the Tiger Parents of my friends from Ann Arbor, where I grew up. Well, that's not saying much. All it ruled out was the expectation of daily 2-hour piano practice, followed by 1-hour practice on ____ [fill in chosen string instrument, preferably cello or violin], with entire weekends devoted to extra-credit math and physics problems, and reading Good Books to improve one's vocabulary. Aside from those minor specifications, the sky was the limit.

That said, I now realize it was inadvisable, poorly considered, and TOTALLY CRAZY to start having babies without even checking out the lay of the land first, let alone a little practical research and preparation! But that's exactly what happened.

Remind Me Why We Do This In The First Place?

Ummm ... Doesn't Everyone?
Like lemmings! It's what species do: procreate. Talking about it programs us from an early age. "Skylar, when YOU are a mommy, YOU get to decide the rules! How great! Bet you look forward to it."

Love Child
Because you and your partner adore each other. Naturally, you have a child as an expression of that love. How utterly romantic ... *because of all the marketing BS!* We'll show you how irrational this really is, when facing parenting practicalities.

Vito Corleone
Some people get all Godfather about it – planning and worrying about who will carry on the family name! Who will defend the family's honor? Who will care for us when we get old, grumpy, and debilitated by various

diseases? Who will toast us at Thanksgiving dinner in 50 years? Who will even INVITE us to Thanksgiving, for Pietro's sake? Quick, let's have a kid!

Lonely

Life can start to feel lonely when you don't have a kid, because so many others DO – and then those friends drop off the face of the earth! They are no longer available for nice dinners (any dinners, really), let alone drinks, shopping, hanging out, leisurely vacations, and spontaneous getaways. We could go on, but we won't; it's too depressing.

Whoops

Birth control is not perfect.

Helen:

I got married in my mid-30s, and had been watching friends go through the stress of IVF and adoption. Being a "plan for the worst, hope for the best" kind of person, I assumed it would take me several years to get pregnant. My husband and I thought, 'Don't worry, there's plenty of time to get ready for Baby.' After all, my eggs were not spring chickens – okay, that's a tortured metaphor, but you get the idea. Well, I got pregnant on our honeymoon. Yes, really.

Why Have a Second Child, or More?

Bucket List

You know who you are! Friends and acquaintances that were polled responded, "You know, I always had this idea (vision, dream) that I'd have three kids running around!" or "We wanted a girl!" In modern parlance, that's called an item on a Bucket List. So now you have four kids. CHECK. How's that working for you?

Delusional

Those who release more endorphins than is wise when around infants.
Some folks love that baby smell. They can't get enough of cuddling little
people who are too young to go to school, lose their jackets, or talk back.
Objectivity goes out the door – it's as though they have instant amnesia
about the years of heavy lifting that come along with children! The incessant crying, the night feedings, the poop explosions, the potty training,
the nap refusals, the tantrums, the chasing-after and the cleaning.

Eight Is Enough Syndrome

Some people are looking way down the road – populating future family
reunions, weddings, and holiday card newsletters. They're creating their
own little villages. Lots of people to hang with – and you're all sharing
some DNA. Cool! Instant vacation/retirement posse! Book the cruise
ship tickets!

Big Bucks

"We got the dinero to make this painless, and we already have the support structure in place." For 2% types, having a few extra heads in their
multiple homes is basically a rounding error. It's like getting a second dog
to keep the first one company: once you have the dog-walker, dog trainer,
poop cleaner-upper, and the person to purchase and serve the food – the
more, the merrier! In Silicon Valley, it's called The Woodside Four.

Whoops... Again

Birth control is still not perfect.

For Our Relationship

"Seemed like a good idea at the time." Some people thought having another
kid would strengthen their marriage. Hmmm. Dr. Phil has said a lot on
this form of logic.

Most Common

Now that you are a parent of one, you are pretty committed to providing this child with a sibling and potentially lifelong friend, someone to enjoy at home with the family. Anyhoo, 3 is the new 2, isn't it?

No matter what your reasons are or were, it's probably fair to say that you weren't adequately equipped to map out the pros and cons, and make an informed choice. You might have entered into parenthood with less research than you did for, say, buying a car or finding and selecting a job.

Chara:

When I think about the countless casual conversations at parks, play-dates, preschool, and gatherings, it seems like such a given that we'd all have more than one child. What we mostly talked about was 'getting the spacing right' – Three Bears-like, not wanting the kids to be too far apart or too close together in age, or hoping for a particular gender. Very close friends would sometimes discuss having trouble getting pregnant again, or miscarriages. I don't recall a single instance of someone saying, "We're thoroughly overworked, over-budget, and outmatched with just one child, so we're stopping right here, thanks," although it was so true, so often.

Perception and Reality

Parenting is a full-time job. When the kids are below age seven, you're constantly on... literally doing hundreds of tasks, many that can't be deferred for long, or eliminated or delegated, no matter how dull or how much of a grind. You must also be able to tolerate tedium, because a good chunk of these tasks become quickly thankless and boring.

Agreed – taking the long view, it's a uniquely important job. You wouldn't stick to a job like this unless you believed in its importance, after all. But it's still a full-time job! So if you feel tired, overworked, and disconnected from all other areas in your life – you're normal.

* * *

Before You Have Kids

Your concept of parenthood is probably as grounded in facts as UFO sightings, the sudden emergence of crop circles, and palm readings. And who doesn't love a great space alien story or horoscope prediction? (wink, wink) But seriously, invest in a little time with friends who have kids. See what their typical day is like, and what kind of issues they're facing. Dig beneath the surface for the 411. In other words, do what we completely failed to do.

Now That You Have Kids

Ooooh. Welcome to the club. The privileges could use a little upgrade, right? Here, I'll buy you a drink.

Chapter 2

10 Shock-And-Disbeliefs

Helen:

When people meet my relatives, they say, "Yikes, I can see where you get your strong will." That's ironic now, because even as a very young child, disobeying my parents was not in the cards. The furthest I got toward taking a stand for my toddler self was in refusing to look at the camera for photos. Ooh, rebellion! In other words, as a first-generation Korean-American, my upbringing was, well, stereotypical. Good public schools, high academic achievement, filial obedience and deference, and no wasting food or funds. There was no nanny, no sassing or interrupting, and no complaining that you don't like whatever's for dinner. You can see how well this context helped me anticipate parenting challenges in 2003, in the progressive and competitive Bay Area, no less. That's right, it didn't!

1   Your annual nanny/preschool/daycare costs equal or exceed the actual annual college tuition you and your parents paid. Yes.

2   For years, talking yourself into making dinner takes superhuman effort because you will be too uninspired and worn out. You can't psych yourself up to persuade your (very young) kids to eat something nutritious time and again, only to have your work rejected. Yes, even after offering foods 17 times per the advice

books. The entire charade is demotivating, especially after a long day at the office.

3   You'll regularly eat cold leftovers from your kids' plates because you're too tired to whip up your own meal. After preparing the hotdogs/sausages/chicken nuggets/pasta that are (urgh) all your toddlers may accept.

4   Little kids are wholly uncivilized. They can and do successfully resist double-digit years' worth of parental reminders, positive reinforcement, nagging and all-out screaming to shape up. Yes, even your kids from your gene pool.

5   Despite all your efforts, your kid could be inherently difficult. Inclined to aggression. A bully. Defiant. Playing victim. Entitled. Whining. Disrespectful. Argumentative. You still have to keep trying, even if there's no improvement.

6   Uninterrupted conversations of nearly any length are a thing of the past. Check with us in six years, though.

7   You will end up paying for any time you are not directly eyeballing your kids in large, unfavorable multiples. Ten minutes of reading the paper or 20 minutes of extra sleep equals 50 minutes of scraping crayon and stickers off the walls and costs eight months' savings to have repainted. Face it, there's no downtime between morning wakeup and evening to-bed.

8   The following will seem like a luxury vacation: dental appointment, CT scan, mammogram, pelvic exam, colonoscopy, filling the car with gas in any weather. Anything you can do alone is suddenly welcome, no matter how inherently gnarly. It's called "mental space" – a concept you won't appreciate until it's a thing of the past. You think we are kidding? Take it from our friend

Claire's stay in the hospital: "I loved being put under, spending the rest of the day fuzzy-headed, and not being responsible for anything. Another great day was when I had to take my husband to the ER after a bike crash. He was fine, but in the hospital all day. I stayed with him and read the paper at his bedside, and our worried neighbors had our daughter. It was a relaxing Sunday!"

9   You will become so out of touch with current events that voting in a local election will feel like prepping for the LSAT.

10 Having this level of responsibility at all times is *totally* draining! A friend told us she woke up one morning, and realized it was the first time she didn't feel tired – her youngest had turned seven.

11 BONUS: Quitting your job and being a stay-at-home parent is not like winning the lottery to mindlessly relive your youth or retiring. It is a 126-hr/week job with surprising amounts of performance pressure, relentless demands, and no paycheck. That's probably in violation of union standards. You may find yourself cringing at gatherings when every person you meet asks, "So, what do you do?"

Chara:

*My SAHM homegirls were so damn impressive. They held weekly group playdates (translation: **weekly hostessing** duties) and somehow gathered the creative energy to throw special birthday parties for each of their little tikes. Some of the ladies went all out: homemade cakes constructed as spinning carousels, over-the-top themed décor, activities requiring handcrafted materials and detailed preparation, and luxurious goodie bags. Looking back, I can't think how they mustered that kind of energy, and all for wee ones who can't even use the potty. But I do recall how hostesses of the more elaborate events had significant help from their own parents – lucky ducks! This wasn't me, and it may not be you, either. Whatever your case, there's something to be said for throwing a party in your home. It keeps you* *apace with your peers, and it forces you to get the place **organized and clean** – because public humiliation is a powerful motivator!*

What To Say When People Ask, "So, What Do You Do?" and You're A Stay-At-Home Parent

- I'm the COO of an early-stage startup. We're looking for angel investors.

- Nothing, what do you do?

- I'm running research trials on early cognitive development.

- Why, should I be doing something?

- I run operations and project management at a boutique firm. We're currently understaffed. Do you know anyone good?

- Do you have three hours? I couldn't begin to list all the things I do.

Big Changes From "Back In The Day"

Chara:

I figured my kids (ages two through six) would be self-sufficient, playing at home and around the neighborhood, as I did in Pleasantville, NY, circa 1977. For at least a year before I entered kindergarten, I freely roamed the cul-de-sac where we lived. I Big Wheeled down hills at oncoming cars (with the black eye to prove it) and created chaos in unsuspecting neighbors' yards. I also remember specific instances of being terrorized by the older kids of our street – part and parcel of being allowed to run wild at a young age – yet I survived, and it gave me character! During my neighborhood wanderings, my mother got to tackle her own chores uninterrupted, such as dinner, work, and laundry, all worry-free without me. In fact, an official kindergarten readiness question at the time was: "Can your kid travel alone for at least four blocks to a store, school, playground, or to a friend's home?" Heck yeah!!

However, in today's metropolitan and suburban neighborhoods, free-range means kids playing alone in their own backyards, and certainly not in the streets with roaming misfits being fed by random households. Alone in the backyard is a far cry from the captivating thrill of playing "in the wild." My kids never left me alone for a minute to play independently outside. That concept turned out to be just another unsubstantiated parenting mirage.

Helen:
My childhood references were completely outdated. I didn't have a clue how much the world had and had not changed, in all the ways that suddenly matter when you're trying to raise a child: work hours, face time at the office, preschool hours and cost, and commute length. Moreover, I totally whiffed on a few essentials that made it impossible for me to do what my parents had done. First, my dad taught graduate-level electromagnetics (i.e. teeny-tiny target audience = very few teaching commitments), and did applied research. He had flexible hours and a lot of schedule autonomy. My mom was a nurse and preferred the evening shift. So one of them was always home between 8:00 am and 5:00 pm, Saturday to Saturday.

My parents kept my sister and me on a very tight academic and classical-music rein. However, during the summer, after we had practiced our various instruments to my mom's satisfaction, we were allowed to play outside, go swimming and bike for hours with no supervision whatsoever, as long as we came home by dark. So we did. And I think we had a babysitter once, for about two hours. That's it.

What's Changed?

I Make The Money, You Make The Kids

For dads, being a parenting slacker used to be socially acceptable! They could be alcohol-swilling, TV-watching, self-centered slobs as long as they covered the mortgage. Wife would have dinner on the table, kids neatly attired, homework either underway or finished, and everyone well on the road to bath and bed. Farewell to that. Share and share alike!

Don't Mess With Mother Nature

Today, dads are more and more involved in childcare. For moms, this means now you have to deal with training the dads or hope you can deal with each other's way of doing things. If Dad is going to participate, how well does he change the diaper? Feed the kids? Clothe them? With a JACKET for the 5th time! You'll be nit picking and frustrating each other straight to the divorce lawyer.

Benign Neglect

Once upon a time, it was perfectly fine for parents to drink spirits nightly, chain smoke, and serve TV dinners to the little ones, who were told to be seen and not heard. Kids were put in strollers, they napped OUTSIDE the store while you grocery shopped, or were sometimes left in the car to wait. Parents played tennis on public courts with their kid in a playpen courtside. Nobody called the police, Child Protective Services, or – best of all – delivered a scathing, full-volume lecture on appropriate parenting.

Go Play Outside Until Dinner

The "playdate" sure didn't exist when we were kids. Mom pushed you out the door and you played with whomever in the neighborhood. The eight-year-olds watched the six-year-olds and the four-year-olds in the streets and backyards. With the new social fear of kids being unsafe if they are ever on their own, there is no easy way to hang out with other kids unless parents take it upon themselves to continually schedule, transport to/from and monitor "playdates". Who has time to do that, for heaven's sake? Even if you do, good luck finding an afternoon that isn't competing with the other child's gymnastics, piano or lacrosse lessons. What this means is that the majority of the time, YOU are the "playdate".

One Phone In The Kitchen

Today, communication never turns off, thanks to email, laptops, iPads and smart phones, to say nothing of texts, Twitter, Facebook and Instagram. It's harder than ever to withstand multi-tasking pressures, expectations and leave work behind at 6:00, 7:00 or even 8:00 pm. At the same time, family is bumming out that you are not "fully present in the moment," which is the kumbaya way of saying Pay Attention to Us Or Else!

Such A Deal!

The cost of living with children is much higher now, including schooling. Public schools are not free anymore! Also, in today's sharply competitive world, folks all around you are paying a pretty penny for language immersion, sports excellence, and enrichment of all kinds. We used to be able to play foursquare and dodge ball after school – carefree with no adults. In today's society this is viewed as the road to slob-hood. We realize that the embarrassment of extracurricular choices some parents face is partly the result of being financially comfortable. Our own sets of parents landed in the U.S.A. without a dime in their pockets, so did not have to field a perplexing menu of options. Consequently, they didn't lose sleep over this kind of crazy. And at some level, it really is crazy.

This Is The House I Grew Up In

No longer is multi-generational living the norm, laying down roots next to or within blocks of one's extended family. Without this "village," parents are left doing everything solo. There's no aunt or grandpa cooking a family dinner, and no neighbor at home to pitch in when you are sick. And how could they? Those neighbors are too swamped chauffeuring their kids to playdates and enriching their children's lives to help anyone else.

Buckle Up: It's The Law

In previous generations, young kids could walk, bike or Hot Wheel around the neighborhood to get wherever, or all pile in into a car without seatbelts. Now, everyone has to have his or her own government-sanctioned, differently-sized car seat. For really young ones, the car seat needs to be specifically installed in the vehicle, which may require assistance from a state trooper. Can you even fit that number of car seats in your vehicle? Who's going to offer to carpool? Seriously? Each parent ends up taking each kid everywhere, at all times.

I'd Like To Teach The World To Sing...

Since folks are gradually having kids later in life, we are becoming "Sandwich Generations" – caring for young ones at the same time as aging parents. No family help when you most need it, and now you're required to deal with ongoing elderly nursing/caregiving assistance. How do you pull this off unless you live practically next door and have unlimited time and funds? Yikes!

* * *

STRAIGHT TALK: No More Village People

Connecting the aforementioned dots, families are ever more focused inward – caring for our own kids and parents, paying for enrichment, driving them to and from scheduled activities, or 'keeping them safe' within the confines of our homes. Has our culture shifted to a new default setting? We are taking on a great deal individually, rather than as a community, neighborhood or an extended family: it's easy to get burnt out on the entire parenting scene. In addition, there are many more women in the workforce – FINALLY. For two parents employed outside the home, it's exhausting to work all day *and* come home to raise young kids. There's always something you are neglecting or not doing – for each other and for yourselves.

The point is that it's crazier now than in our parents' generation, in so many respects. Please don't compare yourself and your situation to them and theirs.

Chapter 3

Your Marriage: Par-TAY is Ovah

Helen:

In the late '90s, I received an unexpected offer to work at a Bay Area internet company. Up to that point, my career had been devoted to healthcare consulting. Also, I'd been living in New York and Boston among a congenial, tight-knit network of friends. So my decision to relocate to northern California surprised everyone, including me, but evidently it was time for a change, and that's what ensued. I joined said internet company and moved to the Peninsula. A year later, the internet company got bought, so I went to a software startup and moved to San Francisco. And during this last maneuver, I was introduced to my future husband Crick on a blind date, engineered by a mutual friend via – what else – email.

I fell in love with his intelligence, lack of pretension, and spontaneous sense of fun and adventure. But Crick was also considerate and responsible; the kind of guy who is rarely running late, but calls ahead to let you know if he is. He was also the voice of levelheaded reassurance when I was stranded in my Singapore hotel room during the 9/11 aftermath. With instant messaging as the only practical way to communicate, I fretted about how to gain re-entry to the USA, while Crick trolled for FAA updates and actually figured out a flight plan.

*By the time we were married a year later, I was already spoiled by his cooking – homemade gourmet pizza; his penchant for entertaining – cigars and cabernet; and his love of weekend adventure – kayaking, mountain biking and hiking. We had no other major responsibilities except for advancing our careers: easy peasy lemon squeezy! That's why it was such a **bucket of ice water** when Baby arrived and this seriously awesome lifestyle took an abrupt back burner to night feedings, food pureeing and tussling over who's picking up from daycare tomorrow!*

In the beginning, you're lovers. Everything's romance, dreams, and hopes. Like a VC pitch, it's all about the possibilities. Then you have kids, and lo and behold, you've become the CFO and COO at a quietly underfinanced, somewhat flailing startup – more *Lost* than *Love Story*. This period of family life might be particularly hard on partners who got used to pampering and customized attention from yours truly. Uh oh. Can you spell O-V-E-R? When you're one of two persons in the household who are potty-trained AND have a valid driver's license, you're no longer the recipient of caregiving. You have little ones to look after! Thus, for the surprise factor and impact, we feel that raising kids is a little like having a grenade thrown at your cozy, happy marriage.

The evolution (or devolution) of marriage conversation

Before Kids	After Kids
Call or text each other a few times a day, every day, just for the fun of it.	No time for either, as it is a nuisance. If you want to help, don't text, phone or email. Please get over here and pitch in.
Tell cute stories about each other in the company of friends and family.	Complain about each other in public, or at least at the playground.
"Sure, whenever you're ready. I'll be here reading/ watching YouTube."	"Aren't you finished yet? We're late, and the kids are starting to melt down!"
When you hear, "What should we have for dinner?" you think about a romantic meal out... or IN.	When you hear, "What should we have for dinner?" you reply, "I don't know. What are you going to make?"

Family Bonding Time Starts When Mom or Dad Comes Home. NOT!

Helen:

Cooking became part of my muscle memory right after college. Starting in graduate school, dinner parties became one of my favorite Yuppie ways to bring people together: sometimes as a pre-party to a special event, or as a reason to try new dishes and enjoy them with friends. When Crick and I got married, meal prep became even more enjoyable. Both comfortable and competent in the kitchen, pulling off a challenging menu was easy, and it was a rewarding way to unwind with friends. I even looked forward to breakfasts – Crick was a master with omelets – and on weekends we'd linger over our plates, sipping our coffee and planning activities for the day.

*These pleasant ways didn't survive too well after we had our first baby. By the time either of us got home with him in his carseat, we'd been in bumper-to-bumper traffic for an hour, thoroughly stressed about reaching daycare before Closing Time, and hungry and tired from our respective workdays. Baby was hungry and tired from his day too, and typically made that crystal clear **all the way home**. So here we were, day after day: three people badly in need of a reassuring hug, a comforting drink, and someone to have already dealt with dinner. As a result, let's just say Crick and I didn't feel warm and fuzzy about weekday meals for several years. Gone were the salad days (PUN) of dreaming up exotic menus together; sharing a glass of zinfandel while we chopped, sautéed, and braised; and bopping around the kitchen with R&B blaring as we whipped up our next confection. Instead, one of us would be trying to get the baby or toddler to stop crying while the other rinsed out leaks from the diaper bag(s), washed baby bottles and nipples, heated rice cereal or veggie puree, mashed fruit, and scraped the morning mess from the highchair. To add insult to injury, Crick was the one who successfully learned to burp the baby – not me. When he traveled on business, the rest of the household was in misery!*

What image comes to mind when you think about parents with young children at dinnertime? Family values. Connecting with each other. Telling about your day. Sharing! Enjoying a home-cooked meal, served with love. PLEASE! This is the result of much marketing talent! The authors, you, and countless others have been suckered into believing this is what your life should be like. Do you know what families with young kids call this transition window: when everyone's headed home and hoping for dinner? **The Witching Hour!** Here is the recipe:

- Take one parent in the house: tired, overworked, under-appreciated. Other parent is still at work or stuck in traffic.

- Add two kids, ages nine months and three years, also tired, hungry, and in various stages of trying to be independent.

- Mix in no time beforehand to plan a menu or prepare food.

- Parent in the house starts cooking and is able to get something resembling dinner going for the kids. It's not something the parent wants to eat, but it's something healthy-ish that the kids might accept because they are hungry.

- Parent likely has to cook a couple more things, because at least one of the kids refuses to eat what's been made. Despite the advice called "breakfast is in the morning," we know from experience that this only works with certain kids. Other kids, like some of our children, have willpower and stubbornness that defies sense. Your judgment will have to prevail. Is this the time to hold your ground? Is this worth the battle? Good news: there is no "right answer." Bad news: everyone will judge you, including yourself. Figuring out what to do and how to do it is not always evident or reassuring.

- Stir in a few more stressors: the constant reminders to chew food, eat what's on the plate, not throw food, not wipe fingers on clothing or hair, and to finish eating because we can't sit here all night!

- Fold in bath – sometimes a battle, sometimes not – then stories and bedtime. But it ain't *The Waltons*, as the media would have you believe – no, sirree, Bob. It's a struggle to get the kids from one thing to the next, involving cajoling, then 3-2-1 countdowns, and perhaps bribery peppered with frustration. The neighbors might call the police – it could be exciting! (NOT kidding. We have friends who've had the pleasure of police presence at bath time. For real.)

The Perfect Weeknight v2.0

Before Kids	After Kids
No evening traffic, so you have enough time to loosen up from work before going out.	No evening traffic, so you don't have to pay exorbitant daycare penalties for being late, plus manage the emotional tsunami from your child, also known as, "Mommy/Daddy, where have you been?"
Sipping a fun new cocktail at a bar with a hip pre-dinner scene and chatting up the 'mixologist'.	Finding something, anything, drinkable in the fridge.
Tweeting that you're at a fab new eatery, then trying something exotic on the menu.	Defrosting pureed food for your little one, and microwaving something instant for yourself, all the while enjoying 2-Buck-Chuck or a Bud.
Hanging out over a leisurely meal, talking about work, friends, weekend, and even posting a photo of you and friends at dinner on Instagram.	Child actually eats food without fuss. No spitting it out or throwing food for fun. You are even able to eat your OWN dinner in between giving your kid her/his spoonfuls.

Before Kids	After Kids
Return home – cocktailed, fed, and relaxed. Change into comfy PJs, listen to music, watch a little Netflix, hit the sack. Ready for another day.	Nobody pees or poops in the bath. No complaining or struggling during shampoo and rinse. Child actually cooperates during stuff-into-PJ time and falls asleep after story! Score! Return to the kitchen and dining room, clean up the mess, wash formula bottles, rubber nipples, clean out and restock diaper bag. Too tired to watch anything. Just want to sleep!

This is married life with kids? It's not what the TV shows pitch you about the sweet sanctity of Family Time. Popular media and parenting books talk about being on the same page, and how everything and everyone will fall directly into line as soon as you do a few simple things. Really? Stick your feet in our shoes and check out some typical nighttime battles:

- *Teeth:* Tooth brushing is NOT negotiable. There will be nights when you've had it, the kids are acting up, and you are DONE. Game over. You hold their arms, crank open their mouth, hold their nose, and shove the loaded toothbrush in there, scrubbing away. If you say you haven't, we assume you're lying.

- *Hair:* Same scenario, but with soap and shampoo, as though the use of cleansing products was akin to waterboarding torture. You've worn yourself hoarse, screeching, "Get over it!" The kids don't. While they're squealing bloody murder, you forcibly wash and rinse their filthy hair, which hasn't been washed in days though they've been playing at the dusty playground and rolling on the grass where dogs have tread. What was that? Oh, the doorbell. Must be the police.

- *PJs:* Pajamas are made of soft, fleecy material. Smooth to the touch. Soothing. Comfortably fitting. Nice, right? But guess what? Who hasn't had to practically sit on their kid, grappling with them in a wrestling hold, while pushing their extremities into the bloody pajamas? Why do they resist? Who the hell knows? Sometimes they're over-tired. Sometimes they just don't want the day to end. Sometimes they're just ornery and wanting to make the point that you don't own them. Whatever. We don't care – just put the PJs on! Besides, the police are already at your house, so how could it get any worse? Ask the police officer if he can help with the PJs.

- *Book:* Finally, book time! The climax of the evening. You'd think everyone would be looking forward to this nice, warm, snuggly connection time in bed. NOT! The one-year-old wants Book A, the three-year-old is bored with it and wants Book B. Each kid tries to antagonize the other, while you're reading to them. Huge argument over which book to read first. You're totally stressed. Nobody is enjoying either book. It's way past their bedtime. You're pissed, falling asleep, haven't eaten dinner or showered, let alone cleaned up the kitchen. So, lower your expectations. Don't worry, all your friends with young kids have gone through the same thing.

- *Bed:* Let's not forget the mounting tension between you and your partner, which is probably at a full boil by now. You have been trying to get the kids into bed and sleeping. Partner is managing matters in his or her Own Way, which isn't Your Way. Now both you and your partner are exasperated and irritated at each other for not being able to "make things happen and get bedtime into a smoothly running process!"

When your partner is traveling on business

Before Kids	After Kids
You know EXACTLY where your beloved is, at which hotel, in what city, on what nights.	With Google Latitude, Foursquare and Twitter, those details are irrelevant. Is her flight scheduled for an on-time arrival, so she can put the kids to sleep?
Loving chats or texts about the trip. How is the city? What kind of food did you have? Is the wine good? Should we go together sometime?	Can't even feign interest. I'm flying solo until you get home. It's all I can do to deal with school dropoff, pickup, and manage my workload at the office. Who cares what you ate?
Will you be visiting our wonderful friends, Jane and Bill, while in that city? Are you taking in the sights? Having a little quality time?	Just the thought of you having leisure time makes me vomit in my mouth. Get your butt back here and help me take care of the kids!
I can't wait 'til you get home! We'll have cozy romantic drinks, dinners, and sex! Miss you so much!	I can't wait 'til you get home! Take the kids, I'm wiped out. And don't even think about touching me, pal.

Your Ideal Partner v2.0

With the benefit of hindsight, we suggest choosing someone who will be capable, positive and supportive while you're in the trenches together. Forget the "Sexiest Person Alive" shtick. You each need a reliable, hands-on, competent partner with very similar values, grit and humor, who can make a decent living and save money. No whining. The fact is, having mutual hobbies or comparable movie tastes could NOT be more irrelevant for the next 15 years of your lives.

One day we sat down and compared notes on what our contemporaries thought made a great catch before they had kids, and what they'd look for now. This would be hilarious, if it weren't true.

Before Kids	After Kids
Good-looking... in any circumstance	Good-natured... in any circumstance, including when covered in diarrhea or vomit
Ambitious. Easily can handle 60-hr workweeks.	Patient. Easily can handle 60 tantrums a week.
Dresses well	Washes, dries and folds well
Has cool hobbies and accomplishments: heli-skiing, triathlons, speaking multiple languages. Perfect showoff material for my women friends!	Has solid multi-tasking and organizational skills: juggling preschool events, enrichment classes, detailed driving logistics, and always remembers the dry-cleaning. Perfect showoff material for my women friends!
Good at remembering my birthday, our first date, my favorite color/flower/foods	Good at remembering the kids' schedules, naptimes, mealtimes, and when they last peed/pooped/had an ear infection
Handsome and tall	Whatever

Before Kids	After Kids
Has shared interests	Cooks *AND* cleans
Good dancer	Good baby-rocker and lullaby-singer
Gives excellent back and foot massages, without being asked	Gives excellent back and foot massages, without being asked
Witty and smooth	Goofy and upbeat... to keep the kids laughing
Humorous	Humorous *AND* practical
Athletic	Has grit and endurance. Can function on little or no sleep for the next five years. For example, changing the kid's sheets at 1:00 am after an accident, vomit, or fever sweats.
Hot, amazing sex	Annual sex, on that one night a year when you're both rested enough to consider it

Now That You're A Mom, Typical Pet Peeves With Your Partner or Husband

Chara:

I met Keith while living in Beacon Hill, Boston. I fell in love with his gregarious, perky, quirky sweetness. His California style was so refreshing compared to the Gordon Gekko/East Coast types I had been rolling with. Keith actually took the time to smell the roses! He also put forth tremendous effort to engage me in his hobbies and interests. We scuba dived together, and I dutifully pored over the binders he organized on new USC Trojan recruits. On weekends, we traveled all over the U.S. to see USC games, or spent lazy weekends in bed watching The Sopranos – my Jersey roots! Fast forward to our married life with two kids under seven. Now Keith's friendly habit of chatting up the postman or taking time to enjoy an unhurried shower is annoying, because we are LATE AGAIN for pee-wee football or piano lessons or whatever, and those cost a fortune. His dedication to following football scores – while my hair is afire trying to work at my job, nurse a baby, and manage the household – is crazy-making. If Pete Carroll isn't coming over to change a diaper, then to hell with him!

STILL In The Shower?

No matter how late you are, how much is yet to be done, or how desperately a helping hand is needed, from Within The Shower, No One Can Hear You Screaming In The Kitchen. That's why he's oblivious to you ranting about getting out of the bathroom. Being on the front line for so long, chances are you've minimized your personal hygiene to every-other-day speed-showering and intermittent bird-baths. There's no time for a 20-minute drenching and soaping followed by unhurried toweling. Save that for the next decade, buddy!

Cell Phone Aggravation 1

He has the kids, you need to communicate something to him pronto, and you can't reach him on his cell. Suddenly you go all Glenn Close in *Fatal Attraction*, calling, emailing, and texting thousands of times, hitting reload on Google Latitude like a freak, and finally both texting and calling those who may be nearby him. Imagine how the conversation goes, depending on whether or not you actually reach him. Mmmm. Not pretty.

Cell Phone Aggravation 2

He doesn't have the kids, although he was supposed to pick them up. You aren't able to get them now (which is why he was on point in the first place), and he's not answering his cell. You didn't know you could redial and leave that many messages in 90 seconds, did you? Or text so many expletives?

Zip-A-Dee-Doo-Dah

Schedule? What schedule? We can't be hurried, we're having fun! Bedtime? Nah. Mealtime? Nah. Time to go home? Nah, we're just getting started! Let's keep everyone up for a couple more hours, so they are really cranky tomorrow, and have meltdowns. Thanks, that's a great idea!

"See To That, Will You, Carson?" "Certainly, Lord Grantham."

He has no trouble staying locked in a conversation in public – including eye contact – while kids are fighting, unfed, or playing with something that is about to split their heads open. Perhaps he remains unruffled because he's confident that you will handle everything before it becomes an issue. Ironically, at this point you are so trained to be on 24/7 red-alert, that you come across as ADHD. In fact, you probably cannot stop conducting kid surveillance during any discussion. If your brain is not half focused on whatever kids are in your care, then you are mentally going over all the preparations you need to start when you and the kids return home. You'll find yourself walking around the house trying to accomplish tasks, while your childless neighbor fruitlessly tries to engage you in a brief chat. Result: the general public sees you as a crazed freak on a mission, whereas they perceive HIM as the balanced and collected other half. Yes, this is part of the thanks you get for being the one who's "on it".

Hear No Evil

He no longer hears anything you say, literally and/or figuratively, and particularly when the children are around. Okay, so his processors are probably overloaded. However, you may be seeing a trend. Entire sentences are lost on your partner. In this brave new world, getting anything across requires a deliberate De Niro hand move, à la *Taxi Driver* ("You, Me, We're Talking") simply so he can grasp the words, "Please bring the brown bag into the car." Maddening, we agree.

Making You Look Shiftless

He is consistent about dressing kids in the clothes that are too big, way ugly (sent from aunt Joan), and totally clashing (ok, maybe because laundry hasn't been folded and put away for a year). Still, your son has bed head, and your daughter's hair is reminiscent of Bob Marley, both have dirty faces and hands, and they are at church or a birthday party looking like homeless children. All on your one and only morning off. Is it any wonder you can't take a break?

Busy On The Computer

You think he is working around the clock. But behind that angled monitor, he is actually looking up sports scores, the Drudge Report, participating in fantasy football leagues, gaming and emailing the "brothers" whatever silly internet stuff only they could possibly find funny. The laptop = modern day man-cave.

This brings us to a pet peeve that deserves a Little Space all its own.

Voulez-Vous Coucher In The Guest Room?

Hey, do you sleep with your partner? In the same bed? Every night? Really? Would you cop to it if you didn't, or would it feel too embarrassing? What if you knew that half your friends were sleeping separately? Would that change your answer?

I Can Almost Remember Being Well-Rested. Almost.

When you have a baby in the house, there's no such thing as a good night's sleep, much less several in a row. There's feedings every two hours, which take a surprisingly long time; walking the neighborhood or wearing out your living room rug while rocking the baby to get her back to sleep; or helping the baby through teething pain, usually in the wee hours. Plus, you're vaulting out of bed at the slightest cry and racing to their room at their screams, your neurons permanently plastered on DEFCON 1. It takes years to unwind from this every time the baby turns over in the crib. Outcome: parents, you are two legally-bonded zombies.

Then, baby becomes active toddler. You're following him or her around for their safety, pushing the stroller, carrying the kid for hours. In the park, at Disneyland, to and from the pool, biking down the street, hauling the kid up and down the stairs, going in circles in the yard. Maybe you're dealing with early risers, late-to-bedders, or potty training and the unpredictable 3:00 a.m. stripping-and-remaking-the-bed that is part of the package. It comes to quite a little workout, with unexpected starts and stops. If you're in your late 30's or early 40's, are you in condition to meet this challenge on three hours of sleep per night?

Also, let us not forget your child's emotional, cognitive, and cultural development – the gold mine of possibilities that parenting articles constantly tout. Are you doing enough for your kid? Singing, music, reading, going to museums and zoos, sensory development and foreign languages? Despite yourself, you begin comparing your kid to others, entering a slipstream of self-induced stress. Your objective brain has shut down, as it hasn't gotten proper sleep for at least a year. Before you know it, you've signed up little two-year-old Andrew for Music Together, Montessori-based Czechoslovakian Sign Language Immersion, and advanced fencing lessons. Outcome: you still haven't slept, you're whipped from parenting activities, you've had no mental downtime, and are now in debt from enrolling your child in extra classes.

But wait, there's more! You have a second child, or maybe a third. Let's do the math. You and your partner have mega-fatigue, and it's compounded daily. Add to that a little aging, a little weight gain, a little slack in the muscle tone around the neck, and you have a recipe for Olympic-caliber snoring. You will probably resort to shoving, pinching, holding your partner's nose, recording the louder-than-life sounds on your phone and playing them back. Do you remember fighting about snoring before you had the kids? Did it get worse over time, or is it simply more annoying because you're so weary and can't handle any more nuisances in your life?

Guess what? Some parents found a solution, which few will admit to: they sleep in separate bedrooms at least once a week. Honest, it is not only Queen Elizabeth who doesn't shack up with Prince Phillip every night. Check with your neighbors. Give them a bottle of wine to loosen their tongues. *In vino veritas!*

Helen:

My husband Crick gets a Lifetime Pass on snoring. I'm the family narcoleptic, and he's the heroic one whose internal high-performance-alert system would jolt him awake when the kids would mutter, cough or cry in the wee hours. It's questionable whether our kids would have survived if it had been up to me. I routinely fell asleep holding our first child in the rocker during nighttime feedings, and he would be the one to make sure I didn't drop him on the floor. He also did the majority of oh-dark-hundred bottles and diaper changes because I would sleep through the alarm. Snoring? What snoring?

Now That You're A Dad, Typical Pet Peeves With Your Wife

NOT ENOUGH SEX.

Now That You're Parents, A Common Pet Peeve With Each Other

Little Differences = A Lot Of Annoyance

When the kids are very young, one way to maintain sanity is to understand their personalities, quirks, and developmental stages and then establish appropriate routines and habits that help everyone function, with predictability. The primary caregiver is a wonderful source of much detailed knowledge and expertise toward this positive functioning. Well, *that* sounds easy. Let's look at the fine print, shall we?

Usually the one parent who is more attuned to the specific rhythms of the kids is more sensitive to the implications of disturbing them. What does this mean? We're talking about the fundamentals: mealtimes, naptimes, playtimes, and bedtimes. If you and other key caregivers (partner, relatives) aren't in sync about these things, it makes for a lot of relationship stress. For instance: "Don't tell me what to do!" or "If you know so much, do it yourself. Otherwise, butt out. I'm doing it my way!"

Not pretty. Actually, it sounds pretty common, and yet the problem isn't discussed in parenting books, except in highly sanitized ways. Most of the advice recommends: sit down with your partner and agree on how you're going to parent, understand your non-negotiables and plan it out. Ah, that certainly fixes things! When does the team from the United Nations arrive to help negotiate and facilitate this multi-year agreement? Who's hosting?

If you and your partner struggle to achieve consensus on parenting, come on in. The party's crowded. Many couples wrestle with these issues every day, though most won't cop to it. Rather, when you run into them at the drug store, they smile and say brightly, "Oh, we're great! How are you?" That bouncy response may leave you wondering why you aren't able to pull your life together, be cheery and on the same page about everything. Don't be fooled. Don't be discouraged. Don't think you are the loser in the neighborhood. Plenty of your peers are enjoying the same messy family life that you are. Behind the double-paned windows, you can't hear the yelling, but the discord is raging in their homes, too.

Which Brings Us to the 30,000 Lb. Gorilla: Your Relationship With Your Partner's Mother

Please hand us our meds. As wonderful as the rest of society may believe your MIL to be, chances are that you and she are merely trying to coexist. Learn to accept her, even if it means you have a superficial, not-so-fulfilling relationship. **Pssst – she may find you even more painful than you find her**. What doesn't kill you or your MIL won't necessarily make either of you stronger, but sure is ripe fodder for cocktail chatter!

Chara:
I spent the first 15 months of my daughter's life feeding her mostly superfoods with minimal refined sugars. I even boycotted the standard cake on her 1st birthday in favor of a healthful alternative: honey-wheat muffins. Then my daughter had her first sleepover ... at her grandparents' house. The next day, I learned that she had breakfasted on a chocolate-glazed, chocolate doughnut washed down with a cup of hot chocolate from the local coffee shop, not the items I had packed! Well, I was beside myself – it felt like I had been punched in the stomach. I was convinced she had been fed poison! Truthfully, looking back, I can't believe how irrational I was. I should have savored every moment of this one day of relief from responsibilities, and shown gratitude to her hands-on, caring grandparents. Sugar be damned!

Your MIL: What You Expected	Your MIL: What You Got
Experienced childcare provider who knows what to do; she's already done it! You are the newbie, ready to learn from her.	It's been years, times have changed, and she's forgotten the details of every phase. Don't expect grandparents to be intuitive with the obvious, including when to feed or change a diaper.
Regular babysitting help; happy to help out when you need it most!	Limited babysitting; last-minute requests are such a nuisance.
Fountain of wisdom during difficult childrearing phases and about discipline.	Annoyance with your discipline methods. MIL's expectations about your kids' behavior are not age-appropriate.
Baby whisperer when it comes to putting the child to sleep.	Has neither clue nor desire to grip the details of naptime or bedtime routines.
Help with laundry, cooking, and cleaning during rough times.	No offers to cook or clean. In her day, she did everything herself. You have to suck it up, too.
Takes the kids on an overnight, so you can have private time with your partner.	Can't muster the energy for an overnight; maybe once every 2 years if pressured. Your kids are exhausting!

Your MIL: What You Expected	Your MIL: What You Got
Proponent of fresh, healthful snacks.	Morphs into "The Candy Man" with the grandkids.
Interested in learning the intricacies of your child and how to care for them in your absence.	Tosses your notes and turns a deaf ear. Anyway, you're crazy (hovering, overprotective, not protective enough, hormonal, mean to her precious son, ungrateful, spoiled, lazy), so why should she listen to you?
Provides extra care and support when you or your kids are sick.	Runs for the hills when anyone in your family coughs out loud, due to irrational yet morbid fear of catching something.

Don't go into this kid thing expecting that your MIL will be taking the grandchildren on several overnights or consecutive weeks during the summer so you and partner can get a much-needed vacation and bonding time. Not saying it ain't out there, but for the most part it's urban legend!

Chapter 4

Where Did The Day Go?

Good Morning, Moms & Dads!

Wakey Wakey, Eggs And Bac-ey

Before you have kids, it never occurs to you that you won't be able to lie in bed on weekend mornings. Of course you can sleep in when you're tired. You just close your eyes, and catch a few more winks. Guess what! Some children at 0-6 years wake up at o-dark-hundred, expect you to be up-and-at-'em whenever they are, and do not like taking NO for an answer, because they're not French, chèri. They INSIST that you get UP and DO STUFF with them NOW. NOW NOW NOW NOW NOW! They don't care if you need to pee, poop, throw up, change your tampon, whatever. If you want to hang on to your lazy mornings, get a goldfish.

Don't believe us?

Tracy Pepoon Ahn on Facebook: "Tracy's new alarm "clock": at precisely 5:45 AM each day, her 22-month-old boy shouts "UPPY!!! UPPY!!! UPPY!!!!!" and bounces on her stomach, while repeatedly smacking her face. No, kids haven't changed her life much at all, why do you ask?"

Stacy Monahan Tucker on Facebook: "I never thought I would actively look forward to the clock springing forward in spring. Then I had kids, and now it means that they'll be waking up at 6:30 am instead of 5:30 am. Yay, daylight savings!!"

Your Morning... For The Next Several Years

5:45 am

Kids wake you. Haul yourself out of bed awkwardly, disturbing your exhausted partner. No snooze button in your life! You get the children dressed in clothes that you had to buy, spray for stains, wash, dry, fold, and put away. Endure arguments about what you chose and a lot of complaining or crying about fit, itchiness, color, pattern, seams and general discomfort. Bribe your way through the socks/no socks debate.

6:27 am

Make their breakfast, which takes several tries. They don't like the oatmeal. They don't like the sausage. They want an egg but not the yogurt, but not until after they open the yogurt and consume one spoonful. No time to put away the dishes or refrigerate the uneaten food. Try not to think about the horrible waste of money.

7:08 am

Make lunch and snacks. Similar arguments about lunch contents, but lunch is more critical, because they won't have anything else to eat at preschool or school. Want to wash the lunchbox, because it's a moldy, filthy mess. They could get botulism from it. Oh well, no time. STRESS.

7:41 am

Pack lunchboxes, projects, books to be returned, show-and-tell item, community snack for the class, sweater that your kids' friend left at your house, and don't forget your child's security blanket or lovey.

7:53 am

Now for the real fun... get sunscreen, jacket and shoes onto the kids' bodies. Not so easy. Try to hold squirming, bellowing kid while applying sunscreen, shouting that they'll thank you when they're 40 and skin-cancer-free. Chase kid around the house, and finally SIT on him or her, rubbing sunscreen onto face, arm and legs. Argue many times about why a jacket, which jacket, who zips it, and if hood must go on or not. Argue about sleeve length (to fold or not fold at cuff), fit, and tightness/bagginess. Why do they pick this moment to channel Heidi Klum about a lousy fleece hand-me-down coat? As for the shoes, tie and retie them, or Velcro and re-Velcro, until the shrieking stops. Go to war about wiping boogers from child's nose. You are successful, but kid is now crying and refusing to further cooperate. STRESS.

8:12 am

So, let's talk about you. Do you have your makeup on, your hair and teeth brushed, your work clothes on, matching shoes, briefcase, laptop, your own work, your own lunch, and coffee? No? Oh well, you're running late! STRESS.

Finally exit the house with EVERYONE'S STUFF. It requires several trips, with bags, shoes and papers crammed into your hands, under your armpits and probably hanging from your mouth. Wistfully reflect that if evolution had continued, all parents would be walking octopi. (For several years, many mothers end up only wearing shoes that can be slipped on and off without hands. From holding an infant you can't set down while clutching a flailing toddler and a car seat, to all this racing about with bags... there simply is no time to deal with a shoe.)

8:28 am

Time to load up the troops. Bribe with gum to stop crying and get in the car. Car seats, seat belts, fighting over who gets to sit where, who holds what toy/book/etc. Got gas? No? Where's the nearest gas station?

No time! Late already. Got to get to work. Drive on, praying the car's gas gauge has a wide margin of error in your favor.

8:42 am
When you get to their school, help unload. Sign in, speak to the teacher (barely), say goodbye to your child. Repeat for each school: kinder for five-year-old; preschool for three-year-old; and daycare for your one-and-a-half-year-old. Punctuate the entire episode with frequent, improvisational remarks, "We're late! Hurry up! Let's move it! Now!" Finally unload all the kids and get them settled.

For parents who are headed to work, remember that after 5:45 pm pick-up from the kids' schools, you will be returning home to the morning mess – and the post-breakfast kitchen disaster will effectively be fossilized and quite difficult to clean.

Helen:

*I can't tell you the number of times I brushed my teeth in the car, followed by a 25-second bare-bones makeup routine. A swipe of eyeliner and blush, peering in the mirror on the back of the sun visor while stopped at a red light. In the years before kids, I loved trolling the aisles in Sephora and Nordstrom, experimenting with beauty products. But while my kids were under the age of six, that stuff so went by the wayside. Instead, I'd grab a few Cover Girl basics in the drugstore while I was picking up more formula, diapers, Pedialyte and Aquaphor. I even remember my husband gently suggesting that it **might be time for a makeup lesson**. That's when I KNEW it was time to get my rear into gear!*

Chara:

Make-up? In this brave new world, there's no longer time for primping. I am just grateful if nobody notices I slept in these clothes and skipped the hassle of putting on a bra today.

Well Into Your Morning (Yet It's Only 9:00 AM)

9:03 am
From the car, call in – LATE – to your first business meeting of the day. Lose cell signal twice, i.e. you're not able to participate effectively. Freak out while on mute. Haul ass to the office, muttering about the heavy traffic. The workday has only just begun. STRESS.

For parents at home, remember, the kids woke you at 5:45 am. Your kids get out at noon. Yup.

Helen:
Do a quick wardrobe check when you get to the office. I once gave a presentation to a large group of physician leaders, only to have one of them point out – during the talk – that I had spit-up milky cereal smeared over my right shoulder blade. Aaaaagh! Must have happened when I was carrying the little one into preschool earlier that morning. She meant it kindly – and actually tried to help me clean it from my suit jacket – but this was hardly the issue that I wanted to be remembered for at work! No, no, no, NO.

9:27 am
Put gas in the car. Never mind getting it washed, though it needs it badly.

9:48 am
Get home, collect car debris – food wrappers, crumbs, banana peels, stray socks, parts of art projects, the bike or scooter in the trunk, plastic garbage bag full of sandy clothes from prior weekend beach excursion. (People with kids will SO understand the state of your vehicle. But people who do not – your MIL, coworkers, boss, partner's boss, old friend – will think you are an utter pig. They will hesitate noticeably before sitting down.) Put all of the items away in the appropriate places in the house and garage. Tired yet?

10:24 am

Clean up breakfast mess. Wash dishes, sweep up food debris, clean countertops, wipe down appliance surfaces. You haven't eaten. Shove leftovers – warm yogurt, cold sausage – into your mouth. Put away the rejected clothes, dirty pajamas and clothes from yesterday. Change sheets from nighttime accidents or diaper leaks.

10:51 am

Take out trash, recycling, and put in new liners in the garbage cans. Empty diaper bins, and reline those too. You're having fun now!

Start a load of laundry. Par-TAY! Put everything away in its place.

11:14 am

Check and respond to emails, birthday party invitations, kids' social events, camp signup/registration, utility bills; renew overdue library books, answer your kids' teachers inquiries. Fill out registration forms; schedule doctor, dentist and haircut appointments. Oh wait – none of these are for you; these are just for the kids.

If any packages arrive, open them, flatten and recycle boxes, and put away items in appropriate places.

11:40 am

Time to pick up the kids! Make sure you have your cell phone, driver's license, car keys. Still not properly dressed, but no time now. Haven't showered. Haven't eaten anything substantial either, but you will have to wait. Find required objects – water, snacks, blankie, lovey, change of clothes, books, and toys – to make kids' commute home bearable. Pack all items in the car, plug in smartphone and race to school so you aren't late for pickup. It's $1.00 per minute for the first five minutes, and $5.00 per minute for every minute after that!

11:56 am

At school, beeline it and grab kids. Careful about making eye contact with other humans: remember your appearance – unwashed, unshowered, and wearing what you slept in. If you can just get in and out (skip the niceties) hopefully nobody will notice. Somehow buckle kids into car, try to mediate arguments about what *Music Together* CD to play, and bring the kids back in one piece.

Mid-Day. Wow.

12:22 pm

You're home again with the kiddos. Deal with what you can of the car crumbs and food debris, art projects, shoes that were taken off in car, wrappers, empty water bottles, mud from shoes.

12:43 pm

Make lunch for the kids, since they never eat well at school. Try to figure out what they will eat (vs. what you think they should eat), and hope you have food in the fridge and pantry.

1:10 pm

Spend 30 minutes trying to get kids to nap. One does, the other doesn't.

1:40 pm

Schedule playdates. Good luck accomplishing this while one kid is awake. Nonetheless, find a piano teacher, a suitable gym class, a soccer team, a t-ball team, a swim class, a music class, and keep finding them year after year, adjusting for your kids' preferences, engagement and skill level. Just kidding! You can't get any of this done because your preschooler, who's awake, wants you to watch him practice taking a poop.

Helen:

Because I worked full-time, playdates were of special importance. They were the go-to occasion each week when I could count on mixing with a few other moms like me, no other agenda except to hang out, and same aged kids. We met regularly on Saturdays and rotated hosting. There was a little something for everyone – picky eaters, hypersensitive overreacters, Lego obsessers, princess obsessers, and stubborn tantrumers. Also, a blessedly low common denominator – I think we somehow intuited an agreement to keep it simple – no fancy hors d'oeuvres or anything that might create pressure. Most of all, we were straightforward with each other. One playdate stands out: the kids were nearing 12 months, and it was a chilly, wet day. After an hour or so of indoor play, the hostess suggested we put on a Baby Einstein video – it was in their heyday, and everyone talked about them as must-haves. We all watched, and frankly, it was downright weird – slowly moving colors, odd music, everything strangely repetitive yet without an apparent purpose. Then our hostess turned to everyone and said, "Is it me, or does this seem like a baby acid trip?"

2:11 pm
Clean up the kitchen, wash lunch dishes.

Your Afternoon. Don't Slow Down!

2:40 pm
Start another load of laundry. Hang delicates. Search for that missing sock – how can there be seven unmatched? Put a second load in, and settle down to 30 minutes of "home art project" with your non-sleeping child. This entails searching for art supplies, setting them up, assisting and putting everything away once the activity is over to prevent disastrous spills and stains. Oh, and scrubbing down the immediate area.

3:20 pm
One kid wakes up – cranky, sweaty and hungry. Your job is to de-crank this child while keeping the now-bushed-after-the-art-project one, who won't go to sleep, from melting down. Tired yet?

3:30 pm
Groceries! Go through your fridge and figure out what you need. Make a list. Just kidding! No time for a list. Both the kids are getting into everything and making a hellish mess with Legos and popcorn. Bonus: amid this flurry of activity, step on a Lego piece in your bare feet, unawares. *Yesssssss!*

3:50 pm
Drive to the store. This is a classic rookie move, because the non-napping kid is *guaranteed to fall asleep en route.* That's what happens when you drive a fatigued kid anywhere, any time. Now you have a decision to make: (a) roll down the windows and let the kid sleep, while you take the other one out of the car and try to "play" together outside, while remaining within 10 feet of your vehicle; or (b) wake up the sleepy kid, and brace for a seriously scary experience. Good luck with that. If you chose (a), be prepared to get an earful from several concerned passersby and the police, wanting to know how you could allow your kid to sleep alone in a car even though you are less than 10 feet away.

4:17 pm
Oh no! Did you remember to pack your reusable grocery bags in the trunk? Curses! Resolve to remember next time, and hope the Whole Foods clerk doesn't give you the hairy eyeball. Over-tired kid is misbehaving and pushing your buttons. Took-a-nap kid is full of energy and grabbing stuff from shelves, driving you bananas. You bark at both of them, earning disapproving stares from many shoppers. You have only cereal, fruit, milk and hot dogs in your cart, but you survived grocery shopping.

4:40 pm

Get a brief, unexpected ab and dexterity workout by lifting toddler out of the cart and buckling her into her car seat in your vehicle, while bracing your foot against the cart wheel so it doesn't roll away; then repeating this move with the baby. At the last minute, remember your bags of groceries – on the last shopping trip, you left them in the cart in the parking lot. Clean everyone's hands using your car stash of anti-bacterial soap and wipes.

Your Evening... Home Stretch!

Chara:

I remember a Martini Mom whom I often encountered in the neighborhood. She confided to me that she hit a wall around 5:00 pm each day, counting down the minutes until her kids would go to sleep. This end-of-day finale was a nightly hell for her. Well! I honestly thought that she was some sort of slacker, uninspired, selfish woman. My impression of her was underscored by the fact that her youngest, a near three-year-old, was sucking on a pacifier 24/7 – really? Isn't Martini Mom embarrassed?

*Today, with two kids, **I fully understand** how Martini Mom got to that point, and I apologize to the universe and her for my being so judgmental and ignorant.*

5:13 pm

Return home, drag grocery bags into house, and unload the children from car. Begin unpacking whatever you managed to buy, while kids create mayhem. Try and escape to the restroom.

5:30 pm

Time to make dinner. Turn on evil TV, so you can cook for a few uninterrupted minutes. Feed kids, stop their fighting, clean up the spills, and start cooking a second meal for yourself, because you detest hot dogs and oatmeal. The kitchen is in disarray, dirty dishes strewn about. Tired yet?

6:48 pm
Partner comes home from the office, asking "Where's the mail? Why didn't you bring it in?" Contrary to pop culture and mass media messages, this could not be further from a "rekindle your romance" moment. No one is interested in a big hug and a kiss. It more closely resembles the changeover between shifts at the parts factory – clocking in, clocking out!

Neither you nor your partner has eaten yet, but it's time to start preparing the kids for bed. Yeeeesh! Go back and read Family Bonding Time.

Repeat… Like Ground Hog Day.

Operational Tip
Think of your car as a mobile locker. Similar to a little MASH unit, it should contain:

- *Hand sanitizer,* right there in the coffee cup holder. Hand hygiene is the #1 single method for preventing the transmission of bacteria, viruses, and fungi. No, your kids shouldn't chug it. As long as it's not used to make Jello shots for the neighborhood, you're probably in the clear.

- *Changing pad.* When they're little, use your trunk as a changing table. It's the right height, private, weather-protected, and if anything gets messy, it's a car trunk, for heaven's sake! Best of all, your kid can't escape or fall off.

- *Diaper bag essentials,* including plastic bags for used diapers and soiled underwear.

- *Gummi-bear style vitamins* for bribery – to stop crying, get in the car, and distract from small but never-ending traumatic events. Yes, you'll feel guilty about bribing. But at least it's not a bag of

Tootsie Rolls. (Helen didn't use these, but in retrospect, wonders if she should have!)

- *Large bandages* (roughly 2.5" x 2.5") and a first-aid kit, including Neosporin and alcohol wipes.

- *Nail clippers* in back seat. Perfect time for mom to clip away, sitting next to the kid while partner is driving.

- Keep *bottled water* in an insulated cooler – such as a soft wine carrier that fits 3 mini pints.

- *Portable potties*, change of clothes, and plastic bags to hold wet or sandy clothes.

- *Back-up everything* – shoes, fleece jacket, blanket—you'll be so glad!

- *Packaged snack foods*, pistachio nuts, pretzels.

- *Kiddie survival bag*, including notebook/marker, mini-bubbles, gum, random toys and lollipops. Take it with you from the car whenever you find yourself heading into a long line or moment of patience that the kids cannot muster. You are ninja warrior now.

Teach your nanny/caregiver/household helper how to check inventory levels and keep the car fully supplied with the above essentials. It will make your life SO MUCH EASIER!

BONUS TIP: Keep a back-up supply for yourself of makeup, deodorant, tampons, toothbrush, and even a razor in your car's glove compartment. Mobile grooming kits will spare you from inevitably embarrassing situations. For instance, while in the throes of parenting two kids under four, Chara found herself on a stage in front of 100+ people, wearing a skirt when her legs hadn't seen a razor for the last decade.

The Best Mother's Day Gift Is To Have The Day Off From Being A Parent

Hallmark and Hollywood put big-time energy into making this straightforward wish seem like a shameful, despicable one. What, we're selfish for not wanting to be the cook, cleaner, logistics manager, chauffeur, activities leader and coordinator, negotiator/diplomat/disciplinarian and emotional mainstay, surrounded by children with sticky hands and bottoms in need of wiping, for one freaking day out of the year? Mother's Day is our one chit, and no cheesy overcrowded brunch requiring reservations is going to trump the possibility of having the day off. But heaven forbid you should say this aloud – everyone will act like you should have your kids taken away from you for good.

Helen:
Ah, Mother's Day: such great intentions, such mediocre execution. I admit to getting a thrill out of my first couple of holidays: I felt celebrated and proud. But when the kids got a little older – between the ages of three and six – I was BURIED from parenting and working, dealing with preschool and kindergarten, facing the rude awakening of no longer having the eldest in a year-round school, needing to find full-time caregiving or camps during the summer, and sustaining the constant motion of cooking, cleaning, playing with and picking up after two active little kids. One year, I begged my husband to take them car camping at a local state park for Mother's Day weekend instead of the slightly pro forma brunch celebration. (They LOVED camping.) He looked stunned and slightly put off – he probably thought I was a real ingrate and misanthrope. I'll tell you what, though: when they departed, the absolute peace in the house was the most thoughtful and desperately-needed gift, bar none. There, I said it.

The Perfect Mother's Day v2.0

At First	A Little Later
Looking forward to seeing what the kids "made" for you at daycare/preschool.	Do I have to keep this potholder/spoon holder/ceramic dish/candle/soap until next year, or could I just take a photo and ditch it now?
Looking forward to whatever he got you in the Tiffany box this year!	Tiffany, shmiffany, please just take yourself to a sleep clinic so somebody can fix your snoring, pronto.
Looking forward to brunch!	Can we pass on brunch, and you just take the kids for the day? I'll eat crackers at home in the glorious silence.
So psyched to get dressed up and dolled up, à la Tory Burch or Theory, for a great photo op with the family! Memories!	What? I have to put on makeup? I just want to eat crackers in silence. Can you take the kids somewhere for the day?
Thrilled to bask in the conviction that you just earned a big medal, lady – for all that slave labor! Rising to every occasion without a whimper!	Don't bother making or building a medal, even if you have unresolved Martha Stewart craft ambitions. If you have that kind of time on your hands, please put it toward FINISHING the honey-do list. Seriously!

The NEW Game Of Life: Unexpected Tradeoffs

Imagine a game that reflects the fluctuating point spread in the early parenting years... your mental and physical capabilities captured on a scoreboard. Each day you earn 20 tokens for a decent night's sleep, and spend tokens when you perform tasks.

For example, for every hour that you are the custodian of one child under seven years of age, it costs you one token. Why? It consumes real energy. When little Madison is awake, you are ON: watching out for her safety, engaging her in an activity, bringing her food and drink, changing her diapers, taking her to the potty (undressing her from the waist down, lifting her onto the seat, holding her so she doesn't fall in, wiping, then repeating the prior steps in reverse order), dealing with her immediate issues, teaching her something basic (like how to put a shirt on), and/or cleaning up after her.

So yes, simply being "on duty" from 7:00 am to 7:00 pm, which is the extent of a typical day with one child, soaks up 12 tokens. If you have a second child, deduct an additional ½ token per hour. Therefore, to accomplish anything else during that day, you only have 2 tokens to make it work.

However, there is a LIFELINE! For every hour of outsourced help, such as a preschool or a babysitter, you are credited 1.5 tokens for two kids. Starting from 2 tokens of capacity, if you can get someone to take the kids off your hands for 3 hours, you earn 4.5 tokens. Now your balance comes to a whopping 6.5 tokens of capacity today. Take a moment to decide how you will spend them. Choose wisely!

Chara:

My colleagues, friends, and family will tell you that I'm a multi-tasking, deadline-driven achiever. Yet, until my oldest turned six, all I did was fall behind in my tasks – day after day, week after week, year after year. My garage was a growing sea of disorganized storage, I had no time for car maintenance (resulting in a seized engine), and my airline miles expired because I lacked time to read any commercial emails or listen to landline voicemail messages for a year! Eventually, my performance at work was affected. Overwhelmed by life's responsibilities, I was a limping-along container of stress-induced cortisol. So what did I do? I undertook a major house remodel. There is no bigger nail than that to seal one's coffin. Of course, that I should have put it off seems like a "blinding glimpse of the obvious," but at the time it felt absolutely non-negotiable.

Cost = 1 token each

Personal Hygiene & Health

- Shower, wash and condition hair, shave and exfoliate.

- Exercise (yeah, right).

- Get dressed in street clothes, blow-dry and style your hair, apply some makeup.

- Take care of your partner. Sex? Meal? Conversation? Remember, s/he's been neglected. Like any good leader, you need to look after the morale of the team. Your partner may be your only backup. Make sure that her/his needs are met. **Tip**: this investment results in a consistently high ROI.

Mission Critical

- Re-make the beds that the kids peed in last night, due to leakage or accident. See *Bed Liners* in Tips section.

- Collect and take out trash and recycling from all rooms in the house. You and the garbage collection crew will be on a first-name basis. Chasing trucks in your PJs every week, arms filled with huge bags of soiled diapers, might count as cardio.

- Prepare a meal. Oh, you'd be surprised what constitutes a full "meal" when you hit this stage of collapse.

Household Upkeep

- Tackle the dishes: scraping, cleaning, washing, drying, putting away. Get used to your house looking like the one in *Silence Of The Lambs*.

- Grocery shop for anything/everything, preferably online to make the most of that 60 minutes. Consider moving food purchases to the top of the list. Google Shopping Express, anyone?

- Do the laundry, 1 token per load: stain removal, moving from washer to dryer, folding, ironing, putting away. (Dear readers, this job consumes four to six hours a week, without fail. Invest in an excellent washer and dryer. See our other Tip about drinking vino on the job.)

- Organize the toys. Consider reducing the number of toys allowed in the home. They stay organized for only 30 minutes, which is a poor ROI. **Tip**: if you can get away with it, save toy cleanup for late afternoon/early evening, and literally sweep them into a corner of the room – **once a day**.

- Organize the garage.

- Gardening (What? You have 4.5 tokens to get you through the day. Don't be ridiculous.)

- One hour of deep housecleaning – vacuuming, dusting, removing kids' fingerprints, window cleaning

- One hour of maintenance of any kind, including repairing and re-inflating bike tires, replacing batteries, inflating toy balls, unclogging a few gutters.

Everyday Requirements

- Unload the car. Put everything away. Clean out the crumbs. (Either get used to the petri dish environment or go to a carwash.)

- Read and respond to email and voicemail. (Maybe next year. Maybe. You can probably handle texts without spending a full token.)

- Handle physical mail: open, sort, read, respond, flatten packaging. (Open the mail? Who picks up mail?)

- Plan and prepare for tomorrow. (Showoff. The rest of us are barely flying by the seat of our unwashed pants.)

- Plan and pack for a family outing. Say, to the next town. Yes, it can take an hour just to mobilize everyone and everything into the vehicle.

Administrative Tasks

- Pay bills. (**Tip**: set up business rules for auto-pay before you go into labor with your first.)

- One hour of errands.

- Scheduling, re-scheduling, entering on various calendars, juggling, remembering and reminding multiple parties about playdates, doctor and dentist appointments, classes, lessons, parties. (You could spend two hours a day on this and never have the workload lessen. Chew on that!)

- Paperwork – filing claims for HCRA/DCRA/FSA, taping receipts to 8½" x 11" blank sheets of paper, faxing or snail-mailing them to some nameless insurance office, following up to make sure they got the forms and that the forms are legible, refaxing when some forms don't arrive, and re-following up; filling out endless forms at doctors' offices; filling out registration forms for any kind of classes – dance, music, soccer, art, gymnastics; filling out registration forms for preschool or kindergarten. (In our insane hometown, we're required to provide proof of residency, such as a notarized deed to your home + utility bills + your last state and federal income tax bill, proving that this is your primary residence and you are paying property taxes on it.) Budget two to four hours every week on paperwork. The only catch is that to be effective, these need to be **uninterrupted** hours. Hahahahahahaha.

For The Kids

- Attend parent-teacher conference. Factor in time for shower/clean clothes. Yes, you'll have to hustle!

- Research summer camps or enrichment classes. (Don't bother. Just ask your friends at the park.)

- Make cards, buy and wrap gifts for kids' preschool friends' birthdays.

- Plan your kids' birthday celebrations.

- Make, buy, and wrap gifts for teachers during any one of these events: holidays, end of year, teacher appreciation week.

- Plan and decorate for – Easter, Halloween, Christmas, etc. (1 token for each hour spent – you will need to budget for several!)

- Shop for kids' clothing. Save money and buy off-season – plan ahead, estimate sizes, and search online during clearance times. Some off-season staples: footie winter pajamas, jackets, rain gear, boots. Find yourself friends with older and younger children, and receive and donate hand-me-downs. You need to save your dough for college, remember? (See our section on Preschool.) Anyway, your kid will outgrow everything in six months.

- Seamstress: sew buttons, take in waistlines, take up/down hems, fix costumes and dress-up outfits, repair the pillow pet with the open seam, do surgery on the Beanie Baby with the little plastic beads leaking out, fix the Playmobile Pirate ship with strings falling off. (**Tip**: think recycling bin. Or prepare to be the curator of a growing mountain of stuff that needs fixing, even larger than the one in *Close Encounters of the Third Kind*.)

Social Life

- Planning adult celebrations: birthday, anniversary, dinner party, family reunion, etc.

- Perform volunteer work — at school, volunteer group or charity of choice for one hour. Includes travel time. (**Tip**: Until you are in a very stable parenting rhythm and have at least 100 tokens' worth of excess capacity socked away, Just Say No.)

Cost = ½ token each

Alternatively, you could choose to spend your tokens on less accomplishment-rich activities. Sample these.

- Take a much-needed nap (AS IF!)

- For one hour, do anything YOU want for yourself – read, watch TV, eat leisurely, massage, mani/pedi, wax appointment. (What? This does not compute.)

- Call your best woman friend, and chat for an hour (Right. Kiss your BFF goodbye as you go into labor, unless she lives in your neighborhood, has same-aged kids, same parenting values, and sends her kids to the same preschool. Talk to you in six years, or maybe on Facebook.)

Cost = 4 tokens each

Below are the ship-sinkers. When they occur, you wonder how you got into this pickle. This is a club you really wanted to join?

- Your partner is traveling.

- Friends or family are visiting you in town -– and staying in your house, expecting to be looked after and entertained.

- You are snowed-in, it's too hot to do anything outdoors with the kids, or it's subzero/pouring rain/so humid your head might explode.

Taken on their own, none of the above seem like a cause for concern, do they? Bad weather – isn't that trivial? Sure... when you're a pair of adults taking care of yourselves. But from deep in the trenches, where you're trying to keep from sinking further while working at your day job as well as parenting kids under the age of seven, *they're deal-breakers*!

Cost = 8 tokens each

- Your computer dies.

- You lose your phone. Maybe you drop it in the toilet by accident, i.e. oh crap – literally.

- Your taxes are due. Today.

- Kid is sick… at both ends. (Always have electrolyte freezer pops stored – make your own in ice-cube trays with Gatorade or Pedialyte.)

- Your partner is sick.

- Your car breaks down or needs major maintenance.

- The water heater / furnace/ air conditioner/ toilet / dishwasher / washing machine / dryer / fridge breaks.

- Anything to do with holidays: Passover, Easter, Independence Day, Halloween, Chanukah, Christmas, New Year's, and birthdays – these typically require extra work and planning. Where's the fairy godmother?

Cost = 12 tokens each

But wait, there's more! Check out these delights:

- The kids get lice. See our section on Lice and how to combat.

- Kid breaks an arm or leg, or has to go to the ER for any reason.

- You're sick, but your kids are not! Who's taking care of them all day? Who's taking care of you?

Helen:

I feel like certain personality types did better – or suffered less – when it came to parenting young kids, and this may be specific to pressure-cookers like the Bay Area, where expectations are off the charts. The Laid Back/ Whatevs would flourish through a blend of obliviousness and laissez-faire. I was deeply impressed by their ability to say, "Oops, we missed the cutoff date for T-ball signups. Maybe we'll try next year," and "Oh, I picked up the kids' Halloween costumes at the drugstore last week – these were on display," without a smidgen of irony. Alternatively, Kraftwerkers made their way by being hyper-organized and ultra-energetic. I was thoroughly intimidated by statements like, "At our last Scrapbooking Night, we picked out the best photos of the town's Easter Egg hunt and added descriptive captions with everyone's name. Then, we decorated each page in a bunny and chick theme," or "I've planned and booked our family vacations for the next year. Plus, I researched all the activities and made sure there were suitable educational and cultural components in each."

My heart wasn't in either camp, so I tried to keep up with things like vaccinations and preschool closure dates, but felt like I was constantly underperforming. After six years of self-flagellation, I got tired of thinking of myself as the proverbial hamster and began to shut out The Voices In and Around My Head. My new standard became: What The Hell, This is Probably Good Enough.

Does This Math Seem Lopsided? It Is.

In a nutshell: when you don't have kids, you get evenings off and sleep in on weekends. On holidays, you can actually recreate and rest. When you do have kids, there's no National Parenting Holiday, like Memorial Day weekend: a 72-hour period when everyone gets to relax. When the kids are up, you're up. When they're asleep, you're frantically trying to tackle the backlog of incomplete life/household tasks before they wake up again.

This goes on 365 days a year. So how do you recover? Well... let's look at that.

The number of hours in a day doesn't change. The fact that the little babies and toddlers can't do things on their own doesn't change.

The only things that can change are the number of (part-time or full-time) caregivers involved, *and your expectations.*

* * *

STRAIGHT TALK

Qualified caregiving is hard to come by! Don't assume your parents or in-laws will sign up for truly demanding assistance or household help. They are relishing being the favored grandparents who get to spoil the little ones. They don't want your tedious list of chores and urgent/important things to get done. They want to play, spoil, and feed sugar!

To those in the minority with helpful parents and in-laws: we are happy for you and we hate you, all at once. But the only way for the rest of us to get any consistent help is to hire it. OUCH. It takes time and money to teach someone the ropes of your children – how to get them to sleep and what they eat. At first you may think, "It takes me longer to train someone than to do it myself, so I'll just deal with it." However, unless you start delegating now, you'll never get off the conveyor belt. If you try to do it all alone, you'll crash and burn.

What to do? Always be on the lookout for good folks and snag them when they are available. That person may be a primary caregiver, back-up babysitter, housekeeper, launderer, neighborhood older kid or parent helper. No one is saying that hiring people to support your family is necessarily ideal. What we are saying is it may be your only realistic option.

Chapter 5

The New Family Budget: You're Broke For Good

The cost of a kid goes way beyond crib, stroller, formula, diapers, and the college fund. So earn big, save up and invest wisely beforehand. Having children is far more expensive than imagined. If you're living in or near a major metropolitan area, you'll probably end up seeking help from babysitters, nannies, daycare, housecleaners and takeout food/ grocery delivery, and all of that costs money.

It's a demanding, challenging, competitive world. Financial experts have drummed into us the need to plan very early for your own retirement and your child's college education. We agree! They just left out one little thing: the cost of parenting kids from 0-6 years of age. It's going to take a mint to keep your head above water. Let's look at some categories of beautifully unexpected, yet very realistic, expense opportunities.

Chara:
Enrichment classes: so much price tag in two innocent words. I thought lacrosse, piano, gymnastics, violin, second languages, soccer, and T-ball came into the picture around age seven or eight at the earliest – when kids can reliably focus and control their body parts. I also assumed

these lessons and activities were super cheap. After all, aren't they group activities with shared costs offered by the local Parks & Rec or taught by artsy-hippie-do-gooders being paid minimum wage? I further figured small businesses sponsored local pee-wee sport teams and paid for uniforms. As a kid, I recalled the corner gas station's family and business name proudly displayed on our jerseys.

Instead, today's group activities have evolved into aggressively priced, for-profit, and paid-for-by-parent "enrichment" classes. It feels like professional development, instead of "doing fun stuff" with the under-seven crowd. Whether you can't afford it or just don't believe in it, go ahead and try to withstand the peer pressure ... it's nearly impossible. You'll find yourself maxing out the credit cards to enroll your kid in three or four of these every three months.

Jeepers, This Is Expensive

- Household Help fund: because, despite all your efforts, the house is a pigsty, and there are piles of laundry to be done.

- Interim post-partum clothing and shoes, for the new you in your new range of post-partum sizes!

- Long-term post-partum clothing and shoes, mostly after you have your last baby. For at least five years, you've been pregnant, breastfeeding or recovering – i.e. constantly expanding and contracting – and now nothing fits. Your closet is full of outdated clothes, shoes, bags and accessories – i.e. What Not To Wear. (See our Midlife Crisis section.)

- Getting Back Into Shape fund: maybe your gym has a personal trainer/miracle worker who'll literally work your butt off so you can fit into your work clothes. Ultimately, this approach is probably less costly than buying several new suits, and healthier to boot.

- Going Out fund, because it's no longer just the cost of recreation and refreshment. Add babysitting fees, which aren't cheap. Why? As parents of a baby, toddler or both, you probably want someone who knows CPR, is mature and responsible, has good judgment, and is really experienced with very young children. So, the friendly teen neighbor charging $8 – $10 per hour isn't going to cut it. Even as your kids get older and more self-sufficient, neighboring teens may not be a reliable resource – many of them, particularly ones who live in affluent areas, babysit once or twice and never return. They have too much homework, too many fun things to do in what little spare time they have, and they don't need the cash. Moreover, childcare is serious hard work! Once a teen brought her laptop when scheduled to watch Chara's kids for two hours. Yes, she thought she'd get her homework done while the toddler and baby played by themselves. [Demonic laughter.] That's why they never come back, and you end up hiring sitters who charge $25 per hour because they are nannies and preschool teachers during the day.

Whaaaaaaaat??

- Childcare fund: especially if your immediate family isn't nearby or available to help regularly. $20 – $25 per hour for experienced people, and it's a seller's market.

- Daycare/Preschool fund: in case you and your partner still have careers. Regardless, you will probably consider a semi-structured learning/social place for your child. It also provides a much-needed break for you – hello, parenting is a 14+ hour work day! $15K – $25K per year, with crazy long waitlists. (See our Preschool section.)

- Young Fives fund, should you decide to delay school enrollment because your child was born in the summer or early fall, or if s/he developmentally requires an extra year. Plan on one more year of preschool tuition, a cool $15K – $25K right there.

- Private school fund, if you didn't buy into the right neighborhood with the really good public schools, or if your kids turn out to need a different type of school environment (smaller class size, "gifted" student program, special needs, etc.). Have fun scrounging $30K post-tax dollars per kid per year.

- (Public) Elementary school fund. It's not free anymore. You must contribute to education foundations and the PTA just to have art, music, or gym once a month. Extras for field trips, teacher appreciation fund, holidays and end of school year gifts for teachers, teacher's aides, principal, administrators, preschool teachers and the like. Extracurricular activities are not free and summer camps are very expensive. So add those in too.

Us? Never!

Rarely do people plan, let alone budget, for kids with special needs, such as physical, cognitive, developmental or emotional issues. Costs include multiples therapies for them and perhaps also the parents and other children in the family, as they try to deal with their stresses. Even for parents with children who do not have special needs, child-raising pressures wear on marriages in today's competitive society. One or both of you may seek counseling just to get through these years and stay together. No joke.

- Therapy fund 1: for the child with special needs, developmental and/or medical issues, or behavioral problems. You'll need this fund for multiple ongoing assessments and therapies. Many won't be covered by insurance. You would not believe the coin required (lawyers and aides to lobby and fight public school systems, etc.), not to mention the emotional and physical costs. $150 – $250 per hour, with waitlists that put preschool to shame.

- Therapy fund 2: for family therapy when you and your child are endlessly butting heads, metaphorically speaking.

- Therapy fund 3: for couples therapy, since you and your partner haven't spent any time on each other for the past five years and can't find anything to say, aside from who's supposed to do what chores/activities related to the kids.

Horrifyingly Expensive Yet Seemingly Required

- College. We're wondering how you will find a way to save over $100K in post-tax dollars, per child, for a Bachelor's degree.

- Graduate school. By the time your kids graduate from college, an undergraduate degree may not be worth much in the global marketplace. Another $100K post-tax.

Absurdities That You're Actually Considering

- Seven- or eight-passenger car for carpooling. You may feel pressure to get a car this size, because otherwise you can't participate with other parents in the soccer/baseball/scouts carpool.

- Four-bedroom house with in-law suite, because three is the new two (although you only have one child so far)... and in upscale communities the *au pair* needs a bedroom, too! You may outgrow your home after you have one or two kids, and you may want to buy in a different neighborhood with better schools.

* * *

Before You Have Kids

Make a ton of money! You'll need to save equal amounts for preschool and college – that's nine years of expensive tuition per child, starting at age three months! Make your way purposefully up that career ladder so you're well above the income and savings waterline by the time you have kids.

Now That You Have Kids

You need to have enough earning power to cover the cost of daycare and help at home. Period.

NEWSFLASH: A Family Vacation Is Not A Vacation

When the kids are 0-6 years of age, family vacation is not a vacation; it's an endurance test. Until your kids are much older or you have a posse of 24/7 nannies à la Brangelina, a family vacation is not R&R, but rather, a lot of extra work. Dragging the giant car seats, the strollers, the bottles; arguing with TSA over the baby formula; dealing with epic poop blowouts in a tiny airplane bathroom; receiving dirty looks and snide comments from fellow passengers; being trapped for hours in a darkened hotel room; having to remain silent, and hoping the little one will nap despite the constantly slamming doors from adjacent rooms. For this, you spend $3,000? Your kids will barely remember any vacation before the age of six. Wouldn't everyone be happier having a picnic or BBQ in your backyard? SAVE the money for a family vacation when the kids are older, or for their college years.

Before Kids	After Kids
Exotic location – the farther, the better	Anything in a one-hour radius
Glamorous and refined – great food, gorgeous lodgings, expensive linens, endless amenities	Down-to-earth and family-oriented – simple kid food, plain furnishings and affordable suite layouts. Preferably with extra cots, cribs and waterproof sheeting.

Before Kids	After Kids
Oceanfront with large waves, snorkeling and in-house infinity pool!	One overly-heated pool with a super-shallow kiddie end for the littlest one. Maybe a hot tub but only if gated and accessible by someone taller than 5'5" with a key.
Peaceful and serene. Privacy. Quiet. Late start to the day... and late end to the night!	Nobody will blink at the amount of noise your kids are making, starting at 5:30 am. But everything MUST be SILENT after 7:30 pm – don't wake the baby!
Happy just being with your Significant Other so you can have intimacy!	You wouldn't consider vacationing without at least one other family with kids of similar ages and inclinations. Otherwise, how will you keep yours from melting down around all the boring adults?
Maybe our parents can fly in and enjoy a nice meal out together?	Maybe our parents can fly in and take the kids off our hands?
Tons of Activities: Wine tasting, bike trails, live music, golf....	Tons of childcare: Does the joint have on-call babysitting? Kids club? Camps? Not a chance we are going without it.

STRAIGHT TALK: You Will Want To Keep Up With The Jones'... But Don't

We're aware that this mostly sounds like First World Problems of the comfortably-off. But it is easy to say that you won't get wrapped up in what everyone else around you is doing. In practice, you will find yourself wanting to give your child the same opportunities. But wherever you are, there will always be someone with more than you. So choose carefully and hang out with families of means and values similar to yours. Ignore all the gossip about what your kid "has to do" or "has to have". La-la-la-la-la-la-I-can't-hear-you!

Chapter 6

Preschool Is A Racket

The hype around preschool is thick. As with wedding and baby industries, it's all about marketing. A story is created about what you "have to have" and the indescribable losses your children will suffer for their entire lives if they don't go to the best preschool, which conveniently requires a $200 application fee and $24K annual tuition. That's right, folks. Preschool not only costs as much as college, but parents buy their way in through status, connections, and cash. Let's also remember: preschool is an organization largely for teeny little kids who CANNOT USE A TOILET YET. None of them can read, write or spell, and many of them cannot speak coherently.

Consider the following actual comments about preschools. Snicker away but you'll find yourself thinking these, if not saying them aloud:

- "Should we go with Spanish, French, or German immersion? Is there a Mandarin Montessori?"

- "Is it better to bring up donations in the application, or during the 1:1?"

- "Oh my god, Jack (*the 18-month-old*) doesn't interview well!"

- "Should I wear this season's Louis Vuitton to the shadow day, or will that look too dressy?"

- "Because of your well-thought-out program, we can be assured that our kids are well positioned for the kindergarten transition."

After parents have put a couple of kids through the reality of preschool, here's what they wish they had asked:

- "How many parents both work outside the home?"

- "Do we have to participate in the co-op, can we buy our way out or maybe send a substitute family member or nanny?"

- "How do families (*not just stay-at-home parents*) get to know each other? What activities are available to build community among parents?"

- "How many days per year are you open?"

- "Is drop-in coverage available on non-contracted days?"

- "What are the hours, and how flexible are they?"

- "What food is provided, or do we pack our own?"

- "Do the kids get their own cubbies where we can leave changes of clothes/underwear overnight?"

- "What's the parking like during pickup/drop-off?"

- "What are your rules and policies for handling conflict?"

Chara:

The preschool admission process really took a toll on me. Due to my work schedule, I needed a preschool that was in session at least four to five hours per day. However, the most coveted (and hardest to get into) offered completely bizarre hours. One was open 2½ hours a day, and the other held afternoon sessions for the overflow of hopeful applicants, which was bewildering. Most three- to five-year-olds nap in the afternoon, so how exactly is this helpful? It just showed how the preschools had parents over a barrel. Demand for specific preschools is so strong that you might find yourself considering moving to a new town if you don't make the cut! It took me several years to get my kids accepted into the hot preschools. Until then, I'd change the subject at cocktail parties when asked the dreaded question, "What preschool do you attend?"

When it comes to preschool, like everything else, Children Are Not Very Small Adults. After years of hard experience and shelling out a lot of dough, we have concluded the following:

- Convenient location and hours go a long, long way.

- A kid's preschool experience is not going to get her into Princeton. Yes, we're sure she's exceptionally brilliant. (That's what we say to everyone, not just you.)

- The main value of preschool is the opportunity for children to socialize and develop with other kids in a consistent environment, guided by caring, observant and fair-minded adults (**not their parents**), who have been appropriately trained.

- The other value of preschool is that parents can get away from their children, and children can get away from their parents. Both children and parents can learn to be with other people and get value from those interactions.

At its worst, preschool is another way for an industry to take money from neurotic people. You're easy prey, and they know it. Let us lower your expectations about the application process:

- It can be unfair, often based on social status, connections, "fitting in," and money. Reminds us of sorority rush plus early-acceptance at Ivies for legacy families.

- It's all about supply and demand. The preschool creates demand when they create "waitlists." Parents feel pressure to apply to every preschool, just in case. You'll either feel triumphant because your child got in, or mortified because your child didn't. By the time your kid is in kindergarten, you'll be totally over it.

- Your social life will stratify depending on what preschool your kids attend. The consistent group of adults in your life (outside of the office) will be defined by the address where your little ones spend their daytime hours learning to use the potty and refrain from biting each other.

- It's normal that as soon as little Junior gets his Apgar scores, you'll send out several applications for preschool. Remember when you thought you were going to prioritize the birth announcement?

TIP: When you find a preschool that you like, get on the waitlist right away. Yes, pay the fee upfront. Remember, it could be months or years before you move to the top of the waitlist. When she was 10 weeks pregnant, Helen received this sterling advice from her amazing ob/gyn (female, with two children). That's right, without knowing the child's gender, and actually, without a baby either; at this stage, it's called a fetus. Understandably, Helen and her husband thought this was overkill, but her doctor was so insistent that they followed instructions to the letter. Looking back, Helen realizes that neither of her kids would ever have gotten into preschool otherwise, due to the length of the waitlists at local organizations.

TIP: If your vibe with the teachers is good, they have direct experience and congenial attitudes with the kids, they assist with integrating your child, and the facility meets all basics plus your budget, then you're as good as gold. Anything more than that – extra space, swishy paint colors, extra fancy toys, etc. – look at it as dollar bills flying out of your pocket.

Sanity Check

If you are tearfully negotiating with your partner to donate thousands to a specific preschool, your hormones might be in post-labor whack. Or if you get a call from a desirable preschool about an opening and find yourself wondering, "What's the catch? Why do they have an opening? Who left? Why?" – just stop. Say YES.

Now That Your Kid Is In, The Madness Continues

Like the baby phase and college years, there is no end to the ridiculous comparisons artfully generated by parenting magazines, books and blogs, to make you feel like your offspring's a slacker. The things you'll hear other parents utter (and yourself repeating) should appall you, and rightfully so. For example, the widespread, absurdist use of jargon. Does that fancy preschool reinforce potty training via multi-lingual immersion, sprinkled with Reggio-Emilia? Or Montessori vs. constructivism? What about academic excellence balanced with whole-child learning? Is there such a thing as partial- or fractional-child learning? None of the kids can read. Aren't we more interested in making sure nobody BITES anyone fatally, the kids are well fed and rested, and the children get to try out a lot of stuff themselves as a way of learning something? Do they listen to/make music? Dance and sing frequently? Laugh like crazy? Hike outdoors and dig in the dirt?

If you associate with a competitive group of parents, you may find yourself getting down on your choice of preschool (as if you had a choice!). Don't give in. Remember: it's a preschool. *None of the kids can open a jar of applesauce unaided!*

Say It With Me ... "Preschool Is A Racket."

- Preschool is nice, but isn't the silver bullet for getting accepted to Stanford. And yes, preschool is terribly hard to get into and outrageously expensive. Go figure.

- Whether they make lunch on the premises and have flexible coverage hours is just as significant as whether they offer Russian/Mandarin Immersion blended with Rudolf Steiner/constructivist learning.

Don't kill yourself over this. Love, hugs, moderation, treating the kids like kids and not mini-adults – if your preschool offers this, relax, you're there.

Preschool Postcript: Age Five Redshirting

After the grind and toil to get your kids into preschool, you were probably looking forward to kindergarten in a nice public school district so you can stop paying $20K in annual tuition. Little did you know that if your child's birthday falls between April – September, they'll be the youngest/smallest/furthest behind/least developed in the kindergarten class. How is this, you ask?

It's all about getting a leg up on the competition. Kindergarten is viewed as one of the early rounds in the tournament. Parents are maneuvering their kids into the winning brackets, which means the outwardly benevolent people around you are working to get ahead by giving their kids an edge over yours. This mindset breeds redshirting, just as in college football, but with children who are working on their pencil grip and using their words. For example, short-statured parents might hold back their son from entering kindergarten on time, so he has a chance to grow taller than his classmates. Oddly, the school system has no rule that you must enroll your child in kindergarten once they turn the appropriate age. Since nobody wants to be the youngest, and the school system doesn't enforce age limits, voila! Redshirting.

The New 'Rule of Thumb'
Let's say the school cut-off date for kindergarten is September 1, 2016.

- This means if your child's 5th birthday is by August 2016, s/he is old enough to enter kindergarten.

- In the past, parents of children with August birthdays (the month before the cutoff) would consider holding their children back one year. These kids would have just turned five when they enter kindergarten.

- Today, parents of children with June/July birthdays are holding their kids back an entire year. Birthday scope creep! That now means kids are more than six years old when they enter kindergarten.

- Moreover, once other parents learn that June/July kids are holding back a year, those with April/May kids start holding theirs back, so as not to be disadvantaged by the June/July group. These kids are near 6½ years old when they enter kindergarten.

- Pretty soon, more than half of the kindergarten class is between 6 and 6½ years old (and creeping up); and some clueless/naïve remainder is around 5 to 5½ years old.

Right.

Five-year-olds and seven-year-olds are often in different worlds, developmentally. How is a teacher to teach this group effectively when half of the kids already completed a year of kindergarten under the guise of a "Young Fives Program"? Is this the desired result? Imagine instead a school policy allowing for a two-month "decision zone". Kids born during the two-month period just before the kindergarten cutoff date have the option of enrolling this year or waiting one year.

* * *

STRAIGHT TALK

Ignore the crazy fuss all your friends are making about getting into 'the best preschools' and hold fast to your principles and care requirements. Be prepared for others' enormous respect and admiration, AND utter pity and derision.

Chapter 7

Work/Life Balance: The Joke That Gets No Laughs

Nowadays, adding kids to your life tips the scales sharply so that "work/life balance" is an ironic contradiction in terms. The situation has gone far beyond wry-grimace-and-a-shrug. Our advice is to forget balance because it's a pipe dream. Instead, embrace altering your standards, letting go, and lots of juggling.

Chara:

Helen worked full-time (versus my part-time status) with two kids under seven. Therefore, this particular chapter has great significance to her, much as the Lice chapter does for me. Brace yourself for deep convictions based on our own experiences – you may or may not have gone through the same!

Helen:

*This subject is my soapbox, and yes, I wish I had a clever solution! In the meantime, here's my commitment: **ask me about work/life balance and I won't bullshit you**. For instance, I will not pretend that it was easy to attend the 7:00 am meeting, because it meant that there was one less parent available to take care of two little kids – a baby and a toddler – each of them needing a full pair of capable hands to get ready in the morning* *and launch their day. It also meant I didn't get to spend that morning with all three of my family members – acceptable on some days and agonizing on others. I will also not pretend that I didn't work my butt off to earn the invitation to that 7:00 am meeting, which included the heavy-hitters in the company. I was proud to have been there, because it meant I'd become a person of influence in the organization.*

Plenty of working women are facing these kinds of challenges, and far harder. I'm determined to create safe spaces to talk about them. Imagine if we all did that for each other, out in the open! No need to keep up false appearances, or have the strain accumulate under the façade!

Is It Me, Or Does This Not Add Up?

Ladies! Now that we are increasingly pursuing higher education and earning graduate degrees, we are a more significant proportion of the competitive, professional workforce. In these kinds of jobs, we are expected to put in long hours. If we choose to raise kids, the new standard includes involvement in the community, volunteering at preschool during work hours (that's when teachers need volunteers – good luck getting your employer to go for that), cooking a mouthwatering variety of delicious yet healthy meals from fresh organic foods, keeping the home clean so you can entertain at a moment's notice, raising children as the primary caregiver, drawing upon the ever-changing new research and science about child development, being "fully present" (whatever that means), being a good wife (whatever that means), and still doing the laundry, buying the kids' clothes, and planning the logistics of their day. We are expected to look good while all this is happening. Moreover, popular media lectures us to "take time for yourself!"

So... how does that work, exactly? Working full-time is really a 50-60 hour week, when you count getting ready and commuting. Part-time work generally means 30 hours per week, factoring in the special hell called email and texts that arrive whenever. Heaven forbid you can't attend conference calls or meetings at 7:30 am or 5:30 pm. Good luck if you can't come up with a professional-sounding euphemism for "I have to pick up my kid from preschool" when you're invited to attend a 7:00 pm dinner meeting that you can't decline without limiting your career in a major way. Typically, it's the mom who is expected to handle all the childcare burdens, with dad or partner as a distant Plan B.

Unless you have a stay-at-home partner, you will need to hire a caregiver to help drive your child to and from school, the park and playdates, while you are getting ready for and are physically at work. During those hours, a mom can plan on being judged by others at the school and in the community for not volunteering in the classroom and at recess, or sitting through the preschool performance of a three-year-old squeaking out, "I'm A Little Teapot." Enrichment classes for children either have to be on weekends, or the caregiver takes the kids during the week while the other moms comment on your neglectful self. This assumes that you earn enough to pay for a caregiver plus the enrichment classes in the first place.

There is this optimistic belief that women can have a rising career AND raise kids, without spelling out how to get there in any practical sense.

In the **1950s**, the tradeoffs were pretty clearly articulated and there was no BS about having it all: "Go to college, get a job, find a spouse/get married, quit job/volunteering, have kids, and raise them."

In the **1980s**, the tradeoffs were not clearly articulated, and there was a mixed message about having it all: "Go to college, get a job or volunteer, find a spouse/get married OR go to grad school, get a better job (no mention of how kids would fit in). " These women were part of the off-ramping that occurred when they got squeezed between professional and family demands. Stop by the corner of Rock & A Hard Place much?

In **2015**, the tradeoffs are still not clearly communicated, and the how-to's are sadly lacking as well. All we have to sustain us is *Lean In*!

Where are the following discussions being introduced and sustained – in high schools, colleges, grad school, our employers and communities?

> *Choosing Your Major So You Can Afford Kids & Still Spend Time With Them During Your Prime Earning Years*
>
> *Effective Marriage/Partnership Strategies To Enable Mutual Career Fulfillment & Child Rearing*
>
> *Plan Your Part-Time, Respectable Career Path, So You Can Use Your Hard-Earned Degree & Raise Kids With Less Guilt*

We are huge proponents of working in meaningful, significant careers outside the home, plus raising children, maintaining the home, and keeping a life. Just know that (a) your life will not feel balanced, and (b) managing day to day will probably require more outsourcing than you anticipated.

Translation: having a career and taking care of your family will call for an independent spirit, an almost overly-confident mindset, tax your managerial skills, and cost major coin.

You might be thinking the best option is for you to work part-time. Surprisingly, the consensus is that while your children are very young, working part-time is the hardest gig of all. In this scenario, (a) you aren't making as much money to cover childcare costs, (b) you're treading professional water, and (c) you are on double duty, constantly toggling between the two efforts that end up greater than the sum of the parts. Being the captain of two ships, you are in charge of most of the details and thus held up to both sets of standards. Your partner and the community have expectations as if you were a Stay-At-Home Parent, and your workplace has expectations as if you were an FTE. No one gives special consideration to your half-in status, and you are feeling super lucky to even have a part-time situation – and thus will perform as if it's your #1 priority and you can keep the job!

The bottom line is that if you want to work while maintaining your sanity, controlling burnout, and having some kind of a relationship with your partner, you are better off hiring full-time help, or else going ahead and working full-time if that allows you to afford 40-hour-per-week household, childcare and logistical help. You might even consider an *au pair*. At first, nearly everyone views paid help as a luxury, but it's far from that. In reality, it's the only way to hold down a job and take care of your family at today's standards.

Helen:
After 25 years of being in the professional workforce, half of them as a typical parent struggling to get all of my obligations in line, it's beyond frustrating that there isn't more broad-scale support for households where both parents work full-time. Some major attention is needed to close a few societal gaps – the kind that can't be filled by Google Glass or 23andme. For instance, school calendars and regular business operations: why are these still so out of sync? Imagine if Safeway or Starbucks did this: "Dear Customers, we're closing all of our stores on June 1st, but we'll look forward to meeting your grocery and cappuccino needs again in September (and then only until 2:00 pm daily). Good luck sourcing your produce, dry goods, toilet paper and java until then!"

*On the more absurd end of the spectrum, but no less a tooth-gnasher: Being The Parent Contact. Why have preschools, room parents, coaches, doctors and dentists assumed that the mom should be the (only) one receiving phone calls and emails with information about field trips, requests for items to be brought in from home, reminders about appointments, and notifications that Junior spiked a fever and needs to be picked up within the hour, when **both parents' contact information** was provided in detail? When the kids were five or six, shortly after I had to create yet another monster spreadsheet enumerating their weekly summer camp registrations,* *start and ending hours, pickup/dropoff/lunch food rules, I went berserk. Or maybe you'd say I went on strike. That year, I listed my husband as The Contact Person on their endless registration forms. (I made myself the emergency contact only.) Oh, it was passive-aggressive, but it was also very effective in redirecting the barrage of inane communications for a time. Share the wealth!*

Q&A

Q: If I want to raise kids, do I have to quit my job?
A: No! But you do have to stop channeling Martha Stewart, reading Real Simple or following anything that suggests you should be crafting everything with your own two hands on the now-mini-organic farm-but-formerly-your-home in order to give your child a "magical childhood" 365 days a year.

Q: Do I have to rely on help?
A: Only if you want to keep from drowning for a few years. There are still a maximum of 24 hours in a day. Without a village, having a career plus taking care of family is not sustainable. Why push water uphill? Even if one parent stops working, you'll probably need additional help for some part of cleaning, cooking, chauffeuring, grocery shopping – you name it. This is based on the assumption that you want to have any sort of a 'life' and be on speaking terms with your partner. The difficulty of realizing your desires is particularly apparent when you have more than one kid.

Q: Why do I feel like I'm the only one who doesn't have it together?
A: Oh honey, because everyone's faking it until they make it. Look, most of us are a hot mess until the youngest hits six, and you start seeing that light at the end of the tunnel. At that point, we understand you may experience a new kind of crazy due to homework, afterschool sports schedules, and extracurricular activities. Maybe that's our next book.

Q: Am I going to feel guilty about working?

A: If you're female, yes, because mainstream media and much of society remain in a seriously old-school mindset. Life will be full of subtle and blatant signals, from glances and eye rolls to hints and comments, that you're a selfish, bad parent. How could you put your child in full-time day care? How could you spend so much time working? How could you want to work professionally now that you have children? (How could you not? At least everyone at the office is potty-trained, can cut his and her own food, and doesn't scream for an hour before napping.) You won't hear many suggest that men should stop working to be good parents, though.

Q: Am I going to feel isolated, particularly from other moms?

A: Yes, but only until you realize they're all struggling too. Start by seeking other working moms who share a similar schedule, pull out a few bottles of wine, and have them over on a Friday night. Initiate or join a weekend playgroup. Make time for these women – they're going to be your lifeline.

Here is our tough-love opinion: you might feel alienated from stay-at-home parents for a while, until your kids get older and more self-sufficient. SAHP lives and schedules are part of a subculture that you can't fully share, because your days are spent at The Office. This could be a new and unpleasant awareness, as you may be accustomed to connecting reasonably well with most women your age. When you're in your mid-20's to mid-30's, you are all pretty much in some version of Being At The Office, so your days are spent similarly. Not anymore. There is bonding that goes along with coffee and playdates at the park, impromptu gatherings, and party and vacation planning in which you are just not involved. These relationships start to crystallize, and if you are out of sight, you end up out of mind.

Helen:

I'll never forget one conversation with a SAHM whose kids went to school with mine. We crossed paths in the school parking lot at morning dropoff and she suggested we go for coffee. I couldn't – I had to go to work. And she drawled, "Oh, you're sooo important, you have to be at the office." I was staggered – couldn't even respond. Instead, I got in my car and cried from hurt and frustration. Never had I imagined feeling so disconnected from a woman in my community, and a fellow school parent, at that. For one thing, I doubted she would have made this comment to a working father in the same circumstances. And since when is it okay to just skip work – to have coffee? What would she have said if our kids' teachers decided to do that periodically? 'Reading and writing are cancelled today because Ms. Doe is catching up with her friend at Starbucks.'

Chara:

I distinctly remember the one and only day that I dropped my two-year-old to preschool without having to beeline myself off the premises to get to work. I was still in my pajamas, and for the first time, paused before dashing to the car. In that very instance, a mom invited me to join their group for coffee. I was bewildered, excited, (and thoroughly embarrassed that I hadn't yet looked in the mirror). So, this is what moms who don't have to be in the office do? I felt like Alice being invited into Wonderland, where the other half magically live. Oh, well. Enough of that. Back to work.

TIP: If you Google 'where can I find a mothers club?' you may be able to find an organized group in your area. Mothers' clubs can offer an instant way to meet other moms, form playgroups, join listservs for gently used baby and toddler gear, and even have social events for dads or partners. Helen doesn't know how she would have survived without the playgroups and instant support structure provided by her mother's club. For years, it was the social lifeline that connected her to other working and stay-at-home moms for advice, company, commiseration – even a book club and wine tastings!

Q: If my kids are in daycare, and I really only need help from 6:00 – 8:00 am and/or 5:00 – 7:00 pm plus some weekends, can't I just hire someone for those hours?
A: If you are able to, **please let us in on your secret**. It's incredibly hard to find regular help who will work those limited time slots as a long-term

gig. Even if you do, don't be surprised if you suddenly find yourself holding the bag, while they take employment that offers longer shifts/more full-time commitments.

Work + Life Is A Zero-Sum Game. Hire Help!

As your job responsibilities expand, the extra capacity needed has to be taken from another part of the equation. You will need to find some other source of capacity as a stopgap. That solution means **outside help**. Good help is expensive. Save now! (Are you getting this "hire help" message? We will repeat as necessary.)

Priorities While Stretched Between Work & Young Kids

Naive Beliefs	Priorities For Your Kids
Perfectly balanced meals on perfectly arranged tableware with perfectly coordinated placemats and napkins	Nothing fancy, regular dinnerware! Pizza, takeout, love, hugs and laughter.
Spotless, coordinated, cool or adorable outfits every day	Weather-appropriate clothes: nothing matches, all hand-me-downs
Starched, ironed, with razor-sharp creases	Clean underwear, just bought at Target because nobody did the laundry. Sleeping in tomorrow's preschool clothes to make the morning easier.
Pottery Barn Kid décor, monogrammed and matching	Sleeping in sleeping bags on the bed because nobody did the laundry
"Mommy & Me" summer lacrosse camp	Kids being kids: drawing on each other with markers and playing with fart putty.

Priorities for YOU	Fuhgeddaboudit
Sleep and health: nap instead of doing email	Hair and makeup? What hair and makeup?
Nutrition of a sort… eating Clif bars in your car on the commute	Barefoot Contessa… who?
Clean underwear, just bought at Target because nobody did the laundry	Spotless, coordinated, always *au courant* outfits
Wearing clean underwear AND reasonably clean clothes	Ironed or starched only if the drycleaner comes through
Car that works: brakes, ignition and steering are non-negotiable!	Car that is clean and organized. Be serious.
Career in good shape. Be well-prepared. Stay awake and alert during meetings, and on top of your work.	Random socializing with colleagues – late fees at the preschool!
Parent network in good stead: Mom's Night Out at your house featuring 2-Buck-Chuck and pizza	Gal shopping, brunches, weekend getaways (a questionable use of time that is too painful to contemplate)

Working Parents Survival List

Now that you have kids, you have two full-time jobs, yet there are only 24 hours in the day. From our own experience, here are our suggestions to set you up through these early years. Focus on the really important stuff. Forget everything else. There's no time for it.

Blocking and Tackling

- Create a routine at home, and stick to it. Phone in the charger. Car/house keys in the bowl. Briefcase or bag packed the night before and propped up by the door. Muscle memory helps when you are exhausted, frazzled or both.

- Makeup bag at the office, and one in the car – both with small hand mirrors. You evolve into doing your makeup at stoplights on the way to work.

- Use personal shopper services at large department stores. Typically they don't charge a fee. Get them to scour the store looking for work clothing on your behalf. Make sure they grab items on sale.

- Get clothing tailored. It is worth the investment. When things fit well, you look sharp and feel so much more confident.

- Feed yourself before you get to the preschool or home. Eat a protein bar on your commute in the late afternoon or early evening. Keep a stock of dry foods in your desk drawer and your glove compartment. When you pick up the kids or rejoin the family, you'll have some personal reserves and be better to handle any grumpy behavior or issues without melting down yourself.

- Find daycare, preschool and camps that feed your kid during the day. Trying to handle their daily meals during the workweek will overwhelm you.

- With your partner, do bulk cooking on the weekend for freezing and reheating during the week. Slow cooker, stews, big pots of soup, batches of pasta with various jar sauces, bags of frozen mixed veggies, bags of prewashed and chopped salad greens. Go ahead, drink a vodka tonic while you're cooking.

- YES to pizza and Chinese take-out as much as required to keep your head above water.

Email Tactics

- Charge your phone somewhere far from where you sleep. Don't read email in bed when you wake up!

- Use email with a good spam filter. Unsubscribe from all the retail garbage that comes to your inbox. Don't even spend the time to open and delete it.

- Set aside time to Delete or Deal, instead of filing or postponing. At the end of the time you've set aside, close your computer and walk away.

- Pick up the phone; don't get stuck in email hell, especially "reply to all" bonanzas.

- Use a Doodle-like tool to schedule things with groups.

- Instead of your own, enter your partner's contact info when filling out registration forms – name, phone number, email address – for school, doctors, dentists, classes, camps.

Preschool/Kindergarten Volunteering – Just Say No

- Only sign up if it's to do an activity you value much more than your actual career and income.

- Only sign up if there's a self-serve website, and if no emails, meetings or phone negotiations are involved.

- Otherwise, donate $ or sign up for something like cleanup after an event – i.e. involving NO meetings, NO convoluted email threads, and NO real coordination

- If you are coming in person to preschool for a performance, a birthday, or some other key event, schedule it as though it were a doctor's appointment on your work calendar. In fact, call it a doctor's appointment; maybe a colonoscopy or a follow-up breast biopsy. That way, when you're rushing around from meeting to meeting, glancing at your calendar, you're more likely to just jump in your car at the appointed time.

Helen:

Talk about an evolution! In the space of a year, I went from Earnest-and-Eager-To-Please Mom who stayed up until 1:30 am making and decorating treats for class party (for a pack of three-year-olds, mind you), to I-Don't-Know-How-She-Does-It Mom who repackaged a container of Trader Joe's cookies in an attempt to make them look homemade, to You're-Lucky-I-Even-Remembered-The-Preschool-Halloween-Fete Mom who proudly unwrapped the Safeway lasagna, plopped it on the potluck table, and thought no more about it.

Staying In Front of the 8-Ball: Gifts for Preschool Classmates

- Your life-saving, money-saving, time-saving website: Daedalus Books & Music.

- At the beginning of the preschool year, count up the number of kids in your child's preschool class.

- Go to Daedalus, and search for some good children's book titles. The Newbery and Caldecott winners are tagged for your convenience. Pick ONE book title and don't worry: even the hardback titles are deeply discounted.

- Buy multiple copies in a single purchase – one for each kid in your child's class, and choose bulk rate shipping.

- When they arrive, open a bottle of wine. Wrap the books individually. On each wrapped book, put a Post-It with a classmate's name. Store in your closet.

- When the birthday parties come around, you can bypass the last-minute, under-pressure, driving-all-over-creation search for a gift. Grab one from your closet. DONE.

Family Scheduling Discipline

- Shared, web-based calendar. Repeat: shared calendar!

- Review the calendar with your partner every week – same day, same time, over beer or wine or both. No surprises!

- ... plus, a 30-day/60-day whiteboard-type or similar calendar for the kitchen, with dry-erase marker pens in multiple colors, to reinforce important events.

- K.I.S.S. Keep. It. Simple. Stupid. Don't over-schedule your kid. When the kid coordination checklist starts to resemble a Presidential advance team's legwork, dial it back.

- Sense of humor. When everything is going wrong, you missed something pretty important for your kid, and you can't get a sitter for Preschool Parent Orientation night, pretend you're in an HBO pilot for "Modern Hot Mess Family."

Bill Payment – Establish Before Kids

- Mint.com
- Auto-pay
- Schedule bank/financial account reviews with your spouse or partner, just as though they were work meetings. Get a sitter if necessary, to have uninterrupted time to go over credit card charges and bank balances. If you have a sympathetic neighbor, send your kid for a playdate and offer to reciprocate.

Laundry – Ugh! Make It Go Away

- Friday night with your partner over beer and wine
- Turn on Netflix or the tube
- You'd be surprised how much laundry you can get through with your partner, and how little it bothers you, when you're drinking beer or wine and watching *Game of Thrones*
- Or… if you have an inexpensive wash-n-fold in town, consider that service periodically

Home Delivery – Your BFF

- Dry cleaning
- Dinner
- Groceries and dry goods
- Clothing, especially sales at Old Navy and Zappos
- Books and toys. Daedalus Books and Music has terrific children's books at remainder prices, with minimal book rate shipping costs.
- Amazon Prime and Google Shopping Express are your friends

Entertaining Strategy in The Early Years – REALLY TRULY SIMPLE

Take the stress out of entertaining. It's more than enough to straighten up the house a little, when your kids are under the age of seven. Focus on being with others. You have years ahead of you to practice your White House State Dinner skills. For now:

> NO party favors, matching napkins, fancy cheese arrangements
>
> NO hors d'oeuvres that require hours of prep and assembly
>
> NO mixed cocktails that require a special shopping trip, hours of prep, measuring, ice chipping, straining and shaking.
>
> NO hair / makeup / dressy clothes that end up being discouraging because they don't fit
>
> NO event-specific decorations if they require a shopping trip, or take more than a few minutes to take out and arrange
>
> YES pizza delivery or takeout and potluck
>
> YES six packs of beer or $5.00 wine from BevMo!
>
> YES veggie tray from Safeway, ranch dip and hummus
>
> YES plug the iPod into speakers and dance like crazy in the front and back yard
>
> YES let everyone help you clean up

TIP: If there is a mother's club in your area, join and make sure you get hooked up with other working mothers. Trade stories and how-to's during playdates and pizza nights. Invest some time in getting to know working parents whose kids are the same age as yours (empathy city), and older (really practical, tested advice) and younger (pay it forward).

Chapter 8

Your Child ≠ A Very Short Adult

Your young child is just that – a child. In other words, a person who is immature, still building knowledge in all respects, without self-awareness or self-control to speak of, and with very little sense of duty or responsibility. Your child has the judgment of a gnat when it comes to understanding how to manage him or herself without falling apart. This is where you come in for the next several years. You're responsible for overseeing the timing and execution of urination, bowel movements, mealtimes, bedtimes and naptimes. Teaching this little person how to respond appropriately to others' actions and words. Helping this young one to cope with weather and temperature changes. Planning all logistics, and providing all transportation. Dealing with the unexpected and, of course, continuous emotional support and coaching. All these are your responsibilities. Why? Because Your Child is Not a Very Short Adult. Between the ages of 0-6, it isn't realistic to think that he or she can hold it together for 14 waking hours per day and suck it up, come what may!

What does this mean? It means you can't live your pre-kids life or maintain your pre-kids schedule. It also means you have to adjust your perspective – A LOT – and your adult schedule to mesh with the needs of the

Non-Adults in your family. You can't pick up and go places the way you did before, because it takes 30-45 minutes to simply leave the house! First you have to pack (bottles, diapers, wipes, diaper pad), get ready (clothes, socks, shoes, jackets, hats, sunscreen), and load the car (baby, toddler, diaper bag, snacks, stroller, Baby Bjorn, car seats, pacifier, toys). You discover that sitting in a nice restaurant, eating one-handed, while soothing an infant, getting up to change the diaper and nurse is just not worth it. There is no Eat, Pray, Love. Your life now revolves around a schedule: Feed, Nap, Sleep (through the night).

SCHEDULE: Oh, Everybody Has One. What's The Big Deal?

As the primary caregiver, you've become ultra-attuned (hypersensitive) to your child's eating, nursing, pooping, napping and sleeping rhythms. Raising a small child is much like taking care of a Gremlin, and you are the one who has to live with him or her, day in and day out. Others don't have such constant heavy lifting, possibly including your partner. *Here is where new parents are easily misled.* You cannot assume Potential Helpers, including your partner and MIL, will be supportive or empathetic to your scheduling wishes. This creates considerable, compounded relationship stress when it comes to the timing of events and pitching in with childcare.

An MIL may be excited for you to join her for a day at the museum or an evening play in the city. But Primary Care Giver might be focused on getting child home by 5:30 pm for a smooth dinner and bedtime. This may not sit well with the adults in the extended family who don't want to be burdened with a child-centric schedule. They don't understand why you won't go with the flow.

Let's look at this operationally. The Primary Care Giver starts planning for a meal 90 minutes before it occurs. What to make, bottles to prepare, how to segue from playtime to hand-washing to settling down to eat, in that order. There is wind-down before bed to consider, plus all the stuff that needs to happen beforehand – taking a bath, reading books, brushing teeth, putting away toys (or clearing a path on the floor so you can reach the bed), last drink of water, potty time or diaper change, putting on PJs, another book, hugs, bed. Mentally, Primary Care Giver is budgeting about an hour and a half for the whole process – after all, the kids are Not Very Small Adults. Let's not forget the possible Moment Of Resistance at actual bedtime, which could be a solid 30-45 minutes on a bad day. Gird up!

On the other hand, MIL and partner are thinking, "It's vacation! It's the weekend! It's a holiday! We're having fun! It's only 8:00 pm!" From their perspective, "It's so rare that all the kids together! What better opportunity to fulfill their every desire than to have Super Fun Playtime? Get them all revved up before they have to hit the sack? How about some candy, too? Sing, dance and wrestle until we're all so sweaty we need another bath! Geez, it's only 9:30 pm, what the heck – keep going, everyone's having a great time!" True dat, but for ONE THING. These are very young children. They have no judgment. They have no ability to prioritize and do what's best for them. They are just in the moment, doing what kids do – taking advantage of whatever's in front of them RIGHT NOW.

The Primary Care Giver has to deal with the consequences of this frivolity later that night and beyond, such as peeing in bed because of a late meal/drinking, or crankiness and missed sleep schedules over the next several days or the entire friggin' week. To them, this approach is irritatingly irresponsible and frustrating – who wants to be the parent who must persuade everyone to stop the games and get with the program? And it's frustrating to the partner, especially in support of an MIL who wants you to stop insisting on specific furniture arrangements, standard meal times and keeping it below certain decibel levels (don't shut the door or slam the cabinet! turn off all electronics!). The Primary Care Giver is not asking for special treatment because s/he is "uptight and need to chill" although that's what their partner or MIL is thinking: it's written on their faces. It's because the Primary Care Giver has to live with these demanding little humans and needs to maintain a consistent schedule because NOTHING else will make life bearable.

And so, dear friends, this is how nightly marriage battles start. It explains many a shouting match between parents of young kids. Hope you have double-paned windows, as they help muffle the shrieks and expletives.

FOOD: Oh, Everybody Eats. What's The Big Deal?

Let's concede the obvious. Parents generally are concerned about their babies' nutrition and health. Only the best for the Little One! At the extreme: growing your own organic white carrots irrigated in Perrier and sustainably-raised heirloom kale misted with Evian. Looking down on those who feed their kids Lunchables and Doritos. "Our parenting style and the foods we introduce early on will make such a difference. She will love eggplant curry with quinoa at age three, and blood orange ratatouille bruschetta at age four!"

Here is where new parents are easily misled. Like using the potty, eating is one of those things your kid can control. You can try and try, but your toddler may be strong-willed and/or gastrointestinally challenged enough to be impervious to your efforts. After all, the "kid menu" was developed for a reason. Who the hell strives to cultivate their palate based on a "kid menu"? Many kids just seem to be inclined toward simple, juicy and fatty foods in the toddler years. Your awful reality might be that Junior will only eat hot dogs and Hot Pockets for months.

If so, forget about Julia Child for a while. Stifle your shame: give yourself a break on some of the meals. Keep offering the fruit, veggies and protein, but be matter-of-fact and for heaven's sake, don't kill yourself or take it personally if it doesn't pan out quickly. Look at your child's food intake in one- or two-week increments, not one day or one meal. Yes, you will have less control than you expected. Parents who have succeeded the most in feeding their kids healthy foods often also have the good fortune of having kids who are fairly cooperative eaters.

Stacy Monahan Tucker on Facebook: "This blog quote below is awesome, and exactly how I've been feeling from *Confessions of a Mother and a Chef Blog*: 'I love my kids more than any mother ever has, and I feed them chicken nuggets, pizza, milkshakes & French fries. I'm ok with that.' I SWORE I wouldn't be a mom who fed her kid junk food; I would give my kid tons of vegetables and international foods. And I did, in pureed form, until he was old enough to voice a preference. And now he refuses to eat all vegetables and wants hamburgers, fries, ketchup, chips, and milkshakes."

Chara:

I called our pediatrician's office when my five-month-old daughter clearly wanted to try some solid food. The advice nurse took a stern position against this route, because 'the pediatric board' stated that parents should wait until the baby is <u>at least six months</u> of age before introducing solids. So, I followed the directive, all the while tormented over denying my baby the food that she obviously wanted to try. Concurrently, a friend of mine with a baby the same age was arguing with her own mother over the very same pediatric recommendation. According to the grandmother, the norm in her day was to feed bacon to four-month-olds! She couldn't understand the delay. Fast-forward a couple of years: the same pediatrician's office changed their recommendations, stating that my second baby indeed could be introduced to solids as early as four months of age. Who really is the expert and authority amid changing research and societal norms? It's either trust your instincts or play Whack-A-Mole? Thanks a lot.

SLEEP: Oh, Everybody Sleeps. What's The Big Deal?

Doesn't everyone just lie down and sleep when they need it? Why all the fuss about bedtime? We assumed our kids would just... go to sleep. Right?

Here is where new parents get misled. Kids often refuse to go to bed at the times when they need it most; and further, they refuse to sleep when YOU need it most. The fact is, your days are made or broken by if/when/ how your kid sleeps. Primary Care Givers are deeply vested in the kid's sleep schedule, as it is their only break for the day. It also dictates the day's pace and tone: whether the kid makes it through a playdate without a nuclear meltdown or early dinner with friends. You need them to hold it together during the Halloween party or their cousin's First Communion, and this requires them to have had a good night's sleep.

Kids Who Sleep 9 Hours vs. Those Who Sleep 12 Hours

The difference between children who sleep a lot vs. those who sleep little casts a long shadow on the Primary Care Giver's life. Like having chicken pox, you can't imagine this until it happens to you. Take pity.

Kids Who Don't Need Much Sleep

If you haven't experienced the pure fun of rising at 5:15 am for 421 consecutive days, you haven't really lived. Some kids actually get up this early ALL THE TIME, like Wyatt Waters and Skylar Burnett did. They don't know that there is a difference between weekdays, weekends, and holidays. Every day is a chance to get up at oh-dark-hundred, and the best way to kick it all off is to WAKE UP THEIR PARENTS with their clammy little hands! This will take years off your total life expectancy. Get those big home projects completed before baby arrives!

Kid Who Sleep A Lot and Like To Sleep In

You are going to be the first and last line of defense getting them out of the house EVERY SINGLE DAY until you boot them off to college. Okay, maybe until elementary school. Good luck, it's really fun trying to dress a deadweight three-year-old and pack her off to preschool. It's even more fun to avoid eye contact with the school principal, assistant principal and homeroom teacher, because your daughter is late every day to kindergarten. Be prepared to be unfriended on Facebook by those who have early risers. They may be pleasant to your face, but they actually hate you right now.

On Co-sleeping
If your kid enjoys co-sleeping, by all means keep it going. Do what feels right for your family. You are no less of a parent because you chose not to Cry It Out. Chara went this route.

On Cry It Out
If you decide to have your kid Cry It Out, by all means go for it. Do what feels right for your family. You are no less of a parent because you chose not to co-sleep. Helen went this route.

NAP: Doesn't Everybody Love To Nap? What's The Big Deal?

When you have multiple children, the art of managing the nap becomes just that – an art. You're trying to solve two things that are independent of each other: (1) getting everyone to bed, appropriately tired, AT THE SAME TIME and (2) keeping everyone awake, with appropriate activities, AT THE SAME TIME. By the way, this includes you! *Here is where new parents are easily misled.* It's a lot harder than it sounds. You and your kids' energy levels and rest needs differ, and the timing changes every few months. So parents try to manipulate the schedule. They may want their older kid to take a nap, because it parallels with their youngest sibling's. Or they may not want their younger kid to nap, because it meshes better with their older sibling's daytime activities. Either way, the goal is to get the kids in bed at the same time each night. Yet this all needs to work for the kids themselves, who either:

- Need to nap, and do
- Need to nap, and resist. However, they often fall asleep if you stroll them, swing them, drive around the block a few (million) times

- Need to nap, and refuse (nice!)
- Don't need to nap, and don't

You may find yourself bending over backwards to create and preserve the one-hour afternoon nap, long after your friends and family have Moved On and secretly think you are a freak. What's wrong with a siesta? All those Mediterranean countries have been thriving on them for centuries. It is clear that kids are much more able, reasonable and cheerful with naps, and so are we. Bring them on!

On the flip side, you could drop the nap and opt for an earlier bedtime. This works if your kids will actually go to bed earlier without a meltdown. If you are one of the lucky families whose kids crash at 7:00 pm without a nap, we salute you and are envious that your cocktail hour begins a full 60-90 minutes earlier than ours.

When you're managing the transition from naps to no-naps, remember it is just that, a transition. It's funny to imagine that a kid would go from a lifetime of napping (literally) to NO naps for the foreseeable future, starting tomorrow. It doesn't work like that in real life. Similar to moving from mostly breast milk/formula to solid food, it can take months to get there. Start reducing the number of naps per week or the length of time that they nap. Experiment with it, and stay matter-of-fact when the transition skips around. Five steps forward and three steps back is the name of this game.

Fact #1: Napping is a topic worthy of Ripley's Believe It Or Not. Grown adults have been known to climb unhesitatingly into a crib that seriously won't accommodate them, just to get their kid to fall asleep. We have done it ourselves, and this could be you, so no smirking!

Fact #2: The implications of having non-nappers under five years old are kind of a given. These kids shouldn't be in a car after 4:00 pm. Once in the embrace of the warm padded carseat, they fall asleep in no time.

Frankly, we'd be asleep too, but we're trying to stay awake, driving. There goes bedtime. Let the cycle begin.

Fact #3: Non-napping kids under five shouldn't be in public after 5:30 pm. They can't have a playdate, meet at a *Gymboree* class, and they certainly can't join others for dinner out or at home. They are in overtired-and-melting-down-mode every night, which ultimately constrains when and with whom the family can hang out.

* * *

STRAIGHT TALK: One Parent's Feast = Another Parent's Famine

Whether it's about eating, napping, or sleeping, you might have won the easy-baby lottery… or not. Try to remember this may be quite unrelated to your parenting skills, your genetic makeup (despite what your MIL will insinuate about you), or how hard you are trying. Although totally unfair, parents with easy babies and toddlers secretly think you are a weak, complaining person who lacks parenting technique. But karma's a bitch… just wait until they have their second or third child. These folks won't know what hit them! We have heard plenty of families proclaim, "If we knew it could be this hard, we would never have had Caroline!"

Chapter 9

Nature (7) vs. Nurture (2) – Top of the 9th

As a new parent, you believe you will turn out impeccably polite, academically superior, incredibly popular, healthy-eating, financially successful, emotionally intelligent, motivated, compassionate, responsible, yet humorous children of high integrity who eventually send their parents on annual all-expenses-paid trips to Europe. Right?

Up to now, in your adult life, you may have achieved goals and experienced success through discipline, good coaching, hard work and focus. It is logical to believe that this can be applied to parenting and create enormous success in your own kid. Depending on who you are, "successful kid" could include a few of these: charismatic, peaceful, charming, polite, down to earth, well-behaved, exuberant, socially skilled, genuine, not too polished, academically superior, really into woodworking, really into math, really into art, really into basketball, really into poetry, really into birds, not too bookish, flat-out geeky, quite good-looking, assertive, easygoing, obedient, independent, confident, neat and organized, creative and free, musically inclined, athletically gifted, articulate, always prepared, never procrastinating, optimistic, peppy, calm, unhurried, on time and ready, happy-go-lucky, compassionate, decisive, and always open to suggestions.

From this short-list, take a moment to notice which ones apply to you, and how many. Do the same for your partner.

Now for some gems that are not on the above list. Some of them may apply to you and your partner – we know plenty of them apply to us: careless, clumsy, sloppy, forgetful, distracted, loud, irritable, impatient, inaccurate, easily frustrated, demanding, self-focused, self-pitying, worrier, fearful, tentative, easily bored, sweet tooth, tactless, non-athletic, impulsive, compulsive, bossy, TV-watching, unpredictable, not very academic, frenetic, insistent, wishy-washy, nervous, anxious, bullying, un-PC, domineering, and inflexible.

So the question is, how does your kid seem to be turning out... and how much of it is nature (born that way... can't really take credit/blame), and how much is nurture (your blood, sweat and tears)?

This is a surprising source of stress. Naively, we assumed that if we set up good ground rules and followed them, our kids would come out Just Right, unlike those terrible, undisciplined toddlers or screaming babies at the airport, at restaurants, or in the checkout line at Costco. Our children were going to be So Great, because we were going to fill their little tabula rasa minds with excellent habits and skills that built on their volumes of natural talents and strengths. It's the Lake Wobegon premise, where all the children are above average!

We found that the tabula rasa wasn't quite as blank or as malleable as we thought, which kind of screws up this whole fantasy. It didn't occur to us that babies could be so hard-wired with a plethora of traits, preferences and characteristics. Redirecting nature's direction can be a miserable, losing battle. Failing doesn't necessarily make you a crappy parent, although everyone will be judging you and letting you know, in no uncertain terms. That's why the margarita was invented.

Chara:

Skylar came out of the womb like a hippie-love toddler: highly social, minimally clothed, and definitely anti-shoes. The minute anyone put shoes on her tiny feet, she would take them off – again and again. So, we gave up. There was no splinter, burning pavement, or sharp object that could stop her. She ran barefoot everywhere – on tanbark, hot blacktop – the only non-negotiable was public bathrooms. After some time, the soles of her feet toughened to the point that I'm sure she could have joined a circus act walking across fire and coals. Even so, friends, family, babysitters, and preschools either forced her to wear her shoes (and repeatedly had to put them back on) or voiced concerns. One mom pointed out how her kid put his shoes on automatically, even before stepping into the backyard (BTW, this kid was anal over his shoes, even when he was on the beach). The consistent implication from other adults was that if I would just apply some discipline, then, like their kids, Skylar wouldn't run around like the barefoot savage she was! No, actually, Skylar would just take her shoes off again. Not every parenting battle is worth fighting.

Kids Can Be (Legitimately) Difficult In Their Own Way

This sounds so obvious, but the catch is that you can't know where your own kid falls on the distribution curve until you've had a chance to be around lots of other kids of similar age. So, your "normal" might be someone else's "psycho" and vice versa, on a range of traits. This is the source of much parental angst, self-doubt, and we say it again, self-righteous judging. For instance, some toddlers see a playground and interpret it as a signal to run-run-run to the next county at top speed. Their parents now have them on leashes because the last time that happened there was a four-car pile-up... and everyone else at the playground thinks the parents are abusive.

Yes, Everyone Is Judging You. (Which Means: Check Yourself. Judge Much?)

Parenting may have always been a general opening for criticizing others, but now it's evolved into an extreme sport. From your relatives to friends, to neighbors, to total strangers in line at Safeway, expect lots of unsolicited direction on what to do and how to do it, especially on occasions when you have the least capacity to do so. Develop a thick skin and a selective memory.

Helen:

When my kids were preschoolers, neither would jump in and participate at play dates, birthday parties, or other gatherings with friends whom they saw daily. They'd cling to my leg for 30 solid minutes, refusing to talk or interact with anyone. Mind you, these were gatherings that the very same kids had been wildly enthused about for weeks. My husband and I love to socialize, so we were puzzled and embarrassed! However, as no amount of attention helped and the reticence eventually passed, we learned to wait it out. At these functions, we'd go about our business, chat with other parents, maybe have a glass of pinot, all the while with a kid Velcro'd to one of our legs. Other parents would invariably try to coax our children into joining in, which often just made things worse. Best case: they'd apologize and back away. Worst case: they'd ask what was wrong with our kids!

Nature vs. Nurture: The Dirty Underbelly

	Nature	Nurture
Examples	Child born in whatever %ile for physical coordination, intelligence, social skills, etc.	Taking what they enjoy, or what they're good at (often the same), and building on that.
What it looks like	Your child happens to be … • gregarious / reserved • cautious / adventurous • unconcerned / anxious • difficult / easy-going • sleeping through the night • crawling, walking, potty training • accepting transitions	You and your partner are … • paying for enrichment classes and lessons • providing consistency • finding a way to relate to your child (even if you don't feel it naturally) • applying age-appropriate discipline • clever about teaching approach and methods
How you may feel when it's working …	I'm thrilled that my kid is fantastic at XYZ, but saying 'my genes rock!' makes me seem like a jerk.	Finally, favorable results from all my labors!
And when it's not …	OMG – so embarrassed, so bummed, and this CANNOT possibly be the fault of my genes!	So shaming to know that everyone thinks I suck as a parent. Planning, time, $ and effort – wasted!

Truth be told, we see that the number and range of things about a child that are "nature" (wired at the factory) are significant and dominant, i.e. not to be sneezed at. Working on the "nurture" is a lifetime parenting effort. Many of us only really learn this lesson once we have our second and third child, and realize how much false credit we gave ourselves.

- One of Chara's children is particularly polite and the other exceptionally inclusive. Teachers (who happen to not be parents themselves) have told her what a great job she and her husband did with each child praising their respective traits. Yet, Chara and Keith put in very little targeted time and guidance developing these characteristics. It's just their kids'personalities.

- One of Helen's children is particularly empathetic, and the other exceptionally organized. Teachers have told her what a great job she and her husband did with each child, praising their respective traits. Neither Helen nor Crick can take any credit for this, though! Their kids were just... born that way.

As for Nurture, many of us end up doing whatever it takes to make it work. It's not what we anticipated, it's not what we're proud of, but that's how it goes. And we are uncomfortably aware of what others are thinking, because we remember having a number of judgmental thoughts ourselves. Take a gander:

* * *

Pre-Kids: Chara judged Randi for having candies stocked in her car for her toddlers. Why would anyone introduce sugar pills, let alone have them readily available? They're nearly equivalent to poison.

Post-Kids: P-l-e-a-s-e! Package of bribe candy in the car at all times, morning too, is a MUST HAVE. Otherwise, it would be impossible to get the kids in the car on time and tantrum-free. *Tip: use gummy vitamins or sugar-free gum as the lure.*

* * *

Pre-Kids: Helen judged parents whose babies and toddlers would act up on airplanes. Screaming, crying, kicking the seat in front of them, fussing, whining and running up and down the aisle. Really? Could you be any more inconsiderate and negligent?

Post-Kids: On a cross-country red-eye, Helen's baby kept the entire business class section awake by crying loudly for 5 hours. Apparently, he didn't like the carseat, the air temperature, the lights from the overhead monitors, the bottle, the pacifier, the rocking, the totally ineffective efforts of his parents, or not being in his crib. Every person in earshot, including the cabin crew, seriously wanted to strangle Helen for being unable to silence her baby. Oh, and the Benadryl made it *much, much worse.*

* * *

Pre-Kids: Chara judged Judy for letting her kids drink from the same glass. Chara asked, "But won't they share germs/colds?" Judy responded, "I am too lazy to make and clean two drinks, and this way, nothing is wasted."

Post-Kids: Not only will you have your kids share a drink, but you'll consume the leftovers yourself. Who has time to prepare all that stuff?

* * *

Pre-Kids: Helen judged moms who let their toddlers eat food that fell on the floor. "How unsanitary and disgusting! They should be paying closer attention to their children's health."

Post-Kids: Not only did Helen let her toddlers eat things that had fallen on the floor, she got seriously tweaked if they didn't, because what kind of person would let good food go uneaten??

* * *

Pre-Kids: Chara judged Michele for being rude, because Michele was unable to hold more than a five-minute conversation. Michele frequently would break eye contact, get up to do something, and allow her kids to interrupt.

Post-Kids: Five minutes is an Olympic-caliber conversation for parents with kids under seven. With just one child under supervision, Chara was unable to hold even a two-minute conversation and had no hope of making eye contact with another adult.

* * *

Pre-Kids: Helen judged parents who were reluctant to attend 8:00 am or 5:00 pm business meetings, saying that it would be difficult to participate effectively, as they would be in the middle of dropoff or pickup at daycare/preschool. How inflexible! Can't you just dial in to the conference line?

Post-Kids: Ever tried to conduct a (serious) business conversation at a middle school gym during PE, or a factory during change of shift? That's roughly the decibel level during preschool dropoff and pickup. Also, try participating in a meeting while the teacher is talking to you, other parents are asking you questions, and you have to read and initial the flow sheet that describes your child's activities, feeding and nap times, and anything important that happened during the day. Oh, and you are carrying your child, his or her clothes, bottles and carseat. Ideal setting for laser-like focus!

Increasingly Heard Diagnoses

Before having kids, we'd seldom heard about these developmental conditions. Truthfully, maybe we'd seen them mentioned in articles, but we didn't pay close attention. *We certainly did not imagine any of these conditions applying to our own children.* However, they seem to be increasingly spoken of, if not more frequently diagnosed, and often call for special schooling and therapy. You can't order up a kid that has the abilities, personality, temperament, resilience, and confidence that would make their life easy. You Get What You Get, And There Are No Returns. So be compassionate, respectful and supportive of other parents. You never know what they are dealing with at home.

- Autism
- Dyslexia
- Oppositional Defiant Disorder (ODD)
- Obesity/Eating Disorder
- Developmental Expressive Disorders
- Sensory Integration Disorders
- Developmental Speech & Coordination Disorders
- Physical Disabilities
- Auditory Processing Disorders
- Asperger's Syndrome
- Attention Deficit Hyperactivity Disorder (ADHD)
- Anxiety Disorders

Your perspective on what's "normal" for a child may be heavily skewed, based on whatever you see regularly with your own kids. Don't take whatever little things are going well for granted, and try not to judge other parents who don't have it all going so wonderfully. There are more parents than you realize who have to throw all their energy and resources trying to learn how to parent a challenging child. Be really, really kind to them – and if you are one of them, be kind to yourself. Huge props to you!

Chapter 10

That Thing You're Having... Is Called A Midlife Crisis

Try this on for size. Your eldest is five and you're just starting to feel like you're peering out of the trenches! You make a hair appointment, and take a shower – yowza! Cut to the salon: you leaf through a copy of *In Style* magazine... but don't recognize any of the celebrities, much less the fashions? In an instant, even if you're 28, you feel totally middle-aged, like someone in Mom Jeans.

Welcome to the new midlife crisis: Coming Out From Under The Rock. You don't have your finger on the pulse of what's current, hip, and happening because you've been trying to get your kids to eat solids, give up the pacifier, get used to preschool and not run screaming from the potty. Duh! When you do make it out of the house to socialize, maybe for a football game or barbeque, the people you meet start referring to you as "someone your age", as though you were Rip Van Winkle.

How did this happen? Let's do the math:

Say you have a five-year-old. Perhaps you also have a three-year-old. The brave, determined, or obstetrically organized among us might also have a one-year-old. If so, that means you've been pregnant, delivering, or nursing continuously for the last six years. Your feet probably have grown a half-size or a full size, so few of your fashionable, edgy, or sexy shoes fit anymore. Your body shape may have changed entirely, perhaps permanently. Ribcage, waist, hips, butt, legs – one or more areas ain't what they used to be. And don't get us started on what's happening to the boobs! Enough said.

By the numbers, the last time you had the time, energy or budget to shop for yourself was more than six years ago. Think about what six years is in the fashion world: 24 seasons! Your hair, clothes, makeup, shoes, bags, and accessories are either COMPLETELY OUT, or possibly partially IN, and only if fashion happens to be in a "retro/throwback" phase. In any case, still in need of updating. That's assuming anything other than some shirts and sweaters still FIT. This spawns depression and financial heartache. Who can afford to replace their entire wardrobe, and who has the time or energy, either?

TIP: Get together with your girlfriends, gather up your clothes, shoes and accessories, and set up a few Shop Our Closets at your homes. Draw straws to choose who hosts first. Be sure to include some gals who haven't had kids (or whose kids are much older) and want to do some wardrobe spring-cleaning! Play loud music, dance, drink a few beers or glasses of wine, try on items you can't imagine wearing, just for the hell of it. Sometimes a couple of new (to you) pieces can make all the difference. Donate to each other!

It Creeps Up On You

Perhaps you got married in your late 20's. Check out this sample timeline:

30: Married. Still happy! Sleeping in on weekends, having long luxurious brunches and rounds of golf at fun/glam weekend resorts, with uninterrupted sex and the possibility of a blowjob giving. Culture, travel, friends and hobbies are a big part of your life!

33: Fun and memorable five to six years of marriage without kids. Now you're 33. Starting to try for a kid.

34: JACKPOT! Pregnant! Prepping for the first baby! The glow is on... we're conditioned to think babies are cute for a reason: so we don't auction them on eBay.

39: Life In The Trenches is underway, but nobody told you this beforehand. Maybe it's because it's a cumulative process. Raising babies and children, ages 0-6, requires you to do EVERY SINGLE LITTLE THING for them. And the bar of what you're expected to provide for your child has been raised to an unattainable degree, so the competitive pressure is ON!

41: You're secretly starting to think that your married/family life sucks... because all you keep thinking about is getting a break from it. Can't see how to bring that about, though – there's no obvious lifeboat on the horizon. Wouldn't it be more fun to date, have dinners out, and sex every weekend, while not having to deal with someone who only draws your attention to all the stuff on your honey-do list? Voila! You're in the sweet spot for a midlife crisis.

Happy Partner, Happy Life

Although it may seem like a crude overgeneralization, men need to get a little somethin' somethin' regularly in order to be willing to give a little somethin' somethin'. When he's taken care of, it's a lot easier to get help with all the parenting stuff that needs to be done. Who knows, he may even be cheerful and willing while tackling the honey-do list. Similarly, you've heard the saying, "If the wife is happy, the family is happy." There's a basis for this, because she's often the one holding the family together: emotionally, pragmatically, and logistically.

Putting these together, regular sex should be on your own to-do list. You may think you don't have the time. You may not feel like it, and would rather be alone for one hour of your day or evening. If this is you, then while you're getting back in the saddle, so to speak, you may sometimes feel like the walking, talking, working, driving vagina with which your partner just happens to have a legal relationship, as in co-signing the mortgage and being guardian to the kids. Nonetheless, we advise you to HAVE SEX REGULARLY. Besides the immediate pleasure, think of it as an investment, for future benefit.

Endorphins Matter

We know what it's like to feel overcommitted, overwhelmed, maybe not feeling great about yourself, and wondering how you're going to get your life in control. Our other piece of advice is to exercise, and do everything you can to remove barriers to working out at least once a week, and increase from there. Find a YMCA or gym where childcare is offered, or go when your partner is at home. One hour a week – more if you can swing it – and we promise you will not regret it.

NOTE: as with so many things mentioned already, please don't assume that your workout experience will be the same as it was before you had the kids. The new name of the game is maximizing the very scarce, precious time that you're not on childcare duty. Go to the gym/tennis court/running path/pool already dressed in for exercise. Walk in, exercise hard, and walk out. Too many new parents make the mistake of trying to re-create a schedule that includes two clothing changes, exercise, shower/hair/makeup and post-exercise socializing – chatting with friends for a while, maybe going to Starbucks. Your partner may not sign up for the two to three hours of solo parenting that's called for each time you exercise. Make it easy on both of you and keep it simple! Walk in, exercise, and walk out.

Helen:
My playgroup went on long (LONG) stroller walks at a good clip. Some of the babies even napped during these walks – double benefit! Later, my husband took to running with the jog stroller. We'd work out at the gym pretty regularly. But after Baby #2 arrived, it all went to hell – I didn't exercise for three straight years. Finally, I made myself go to 6:00 am weekday/7:00 am weekend classes right near my house. I sleepwalked to them by wearing my exercise clothes to bed the night before, putting my car keys in my shoes next to the door. True story. Desperate times, desperate measures!

Keith's Law (Chara's hubby) – No Divorce Before The Youngest Is 7

Face it, until your youngest is six, you have no opportunity to be the person you really want to be, get the rest you really need, or put your attention on things that might involve your partner/you/your relationship, without having to address some time-sensitive situation involving the kids. So, you're both wrecks. Be honest! If you're able to shower every day, get dressed nicely each morning, and have 20 minutes of civilized, non-kid discussion with each other, you are already on the medal podium of the Marriage Olympics.

If you are like many of us during these years, you may have thought about throwing in the marriage towel more frequently than you would like to admit. However, once you've made it this far, you may find an easing in the drudgery, energy demands, and frustration. So wait for the youngest to turn 7. Then try and focus on "till death do you part".

The "I-Have-No-Life" Crisis

Date Nights

No-Kid People don't have 'date nights' because every night can be a date night! You relax together. You actually listen and talk about interesting things. These folks imagine life will be the same as before, yet with a cute little rug-rat racing around, magically needing no supervision from either of you.

What **People With Kids** Actually Do: Can you even find a sitter; or afford one? Your so-called girlfriends won't give up any names. Can you keep your eyes open long enough to have dinner after 8:00 pm? Do you have any desire to go out to dinner when you could take a nap instead? Date night? Who needs it? Better yet, how about a full-time assistant and a good night's sleep... for the next five years.

Yes, you should be prepared for a major shift in your relationship with your partner. To those people offering advice about couples getting away for the weekend, we say "Absolutely, as long as you're taking care of the kids while we're gone." It's not rocket science to see that we all need to get away from time to time. However, many of us don't have nearby family who are willing, responsible, agile and healthy enough to handle the kids. If you do, we're officially envious and hope you use them a lot. For the rest of us, once you add up the cost of the 24-hour getaway plus 36 hours of babysitting fees, it's incredibly hard to justify.

Let's say you do find a sitter and save up the dough for a weekend get-away. It is not fun or easy leaving screaming, leg-latching toddlers at home – especially if the sitter is someone who hasn't spent the last few months learning to handle your kid's idiosyncrasies. Good luck finding someone who has the ability to empathize, understand and hold the fort while you're an hour or more away. New parents can easily start second-guessing themselves out of the whole idea. "Is it worth stressing everyone out? Are the kids going to be okay? What if they cry most of the weekend and don't sleep well?"

We offer an alternative to the much needed, yet impractical weekend getaway: a regular **daytime date on the weekend**. Why? First of all, you're both more likely to stay awake. You could simply go on a walk together, take a bike ride, or grab a coffee and talk. Because that's probably what you really need – to connect, and without spending $$. Alternatively, find a thick-skinned family with similar-aged kids and parenting methods and do an every-other week child-swap from 2:30 pm – 6:00 pm!

TIP: Care.com. Sign up now.

Time With Friends

"We are all a little weird, and life is a little weird, and when we find someone whose weirdness is compatible with ours, we join up with them and fall in mutual weirdness, and call it love." – Dr. Seuss

No-Kid People meet new friends through friends, hobbies or work. Go out for drinks, hang out at a party, play a sport together.

No-Kid People THINK that once they have kids, they'll meet new friends in the neighborhood. Plan family BBQs with neighbors or whoever happens to live across the street, and they automatically become your new BFFs. Your sister-in-law is expecting a kid AND lives in the neighborhood – woot woot! The friendship possibilities are endless.

Have-Kid People actually undergo a complex calculus of meeting people and making friendships with families, both old and new. At first, you get married, and you add partners into the mix of your existing friends. It's like *match.com* in multiples of four. You pray that they can tolerate each other, enjoy the same humor, political views, job interests, hobbies, and voila! You're all friends!

Later, you have kids, and maybe some friends or family members also have kids at the same time. Initially you look forward to spending time together. But a year or so later, you are dismayed if your parenting styles, values, priorities, and choices haven't meshed. Perhaps your kids don't get along, because (and this is not atypical) there is one in the mix who is aggressive, demanding, won't share, spastic or won't nap. Maybe that kid is one of yours! Perhaps the other parents are either more lax about the dynamic than you would like; or far too strict with all of the kids. Eventually you realize that your time together is pointless and you stop getting together.

What does this mean? It leaves you with roughly three to five families within reach who easily fit with yours. So, your new definition of friendship will be more or less based on propinquity. In other words, you see each other at drop-off and respond to each other's email overtures for play dates, parenting commiseration, and survival (e.g., we both like to have a martini at playdates), rather than major mojo or common interests. Basically, you had more chance of finding Mr./Ms. Right on Tinder than of finding a family with children of similar ages, in your neighborhood, with whom you all get along.

TIP: If your kid is in an activity like tumbling, dance, art, music – whatever – go and observe the other kids and families. Whom do they get along with? Which kids' parents seem to share your parenting approach and style? Strike up a conversation with them. Meet at the park and hang out!

Sleep, or The Lack Thereof

No-Kid People sleep in on the weekends, particularly when on vacation. They get up when the mood strikes.

No-Kid People have no reason to imagine that they can't always sleep in on the weekends, and definitely on vacation, after they've started a family.

Babies and kids like to sleep in, too – especially after an exhausting day of vacation activity... right?

Have-Kid People don't get much sleep for months or years, depending on how many kids are below the age of four. We repeat: people with young kids – that's you – do Not Get Much Sleep. Yes, you should feel pity for them.

TIP: Hire help, even a mother's helper, so you can catch up on sleep. Yes, we know – this looks ridiculous in print. And if you're like the rest of us, your instinct will be to use any paid-help time to knock a few items off your honey-do list. Resist this urge and TAKE A NAP. The human body needs rest! This is mostly necessary when your child is not yet sleeping through the night.

P.S. If you can't bring yourself to do this because you feel like you must be "doing something" then buy a matinee ticket to a local movie and nap there.

Leisure Time, or The Lack Thereof

No-Kid People enjoy leisure time after work. They get to see people of their choosing; eat what, where and when they want, and chill out in whatever manner floats their boat.

No-Kid People THINK that once they have kids, and said kid goes to bed, it's leisure time! Chin-chin! Bottoms up!

Have-Kid People understand that they are going to be Dog Tired by the time the kids have been muscled abed. And yet, they're faced with dirty dishes, putting away toys, books, and clothes, and probably attending to several loads of laundry. Right. So, say goodbye to your old definition of leisure time during your "work-life-young-kid-balancing" years.

TIP: Folding the laundry while having a drink may need to qualify as semi-leisure. While you're at it, watch a movie or binge on a season of a TV series.

Time with Old Friends Who Don't Have Kids

No-Kid People may find themselves wondering why their friends with young kids don't accept their gracious offers to stay *en famille* at their nice vacation home. Simple: because it's like an eight-car pileup waiting to happen.

Do you really want three alien monsters to land in your beautiful house full of good furniture, expensive upholstery, slippery hard floors, and hand-blown Italian glass vases on low tables?

Do you like to have your Sunday morning slow-wake-up-sex interrupted by colicky babies?

Would you prefer to eat dinner in the mid-afternoon, because that's when the two-year-old has to eat or have a metabolic breakdown?

Are you looking forward to skipping aperitifs *al fresco* while everyone else is seated around the outdoor pizza oven, to help your guest bathe a sobbing toddler and give a bottle to the baby?

Did you envision restraining your guests' kids from climbing your couches, jumping on the beds, and spending the majority of your waking hours distracting them with activities?

We didn't think so.

Dearest No-Kid-People, this is why we don't hang out with you. We may be worn out, but are not totally stupid. We want to preserve what little we have of our dignity, as well as hang on to the possibility of remaining friends. So the straight answer to your question – why won't couples with kids under seven invite us anywhere or hang out anymore?

BECAUSE YOU WOULD SO NOT ENJOY IT.

But please, keep us in mind and call us in five years.

TIP: We have no tips on this front. Seriously.

Chapter 11

Head Lice Aren't Nice.
And They're Probably Crawling
On Your Scalp Right Now.

You have FINALLY ARRIVED. It's Week Four of Kindergarten, your daughter has fully acclimated and loves school; awash in relief, you're ready to coast for a few months! Feelin' goooood! Just then, your phone rings, your email chirps, and a text message 'pings'. It's the school. Get the hell up here and whisk your kid home PRONTO – she has **LICE!!**

Gooooooood morning! Head lice live in every community, especially among young kids – even yours – but few will talk openly about having them. If your child is a girl, odds are relatively high for having head lice by the time she turns 12. Are there any exceptions? Well, maybe bald communities. We've had lice in our homes, and been the volunteer lice checkers in the classrooms. Every year, schools send out health notices with the subject line "Lice Notification". Chara personally identified over 20 cases of lice in a mere three classrooms of approximately 22 kids each. That's a 33% hit rate.

UNPROVEN RUMOR: Lice infestations are on the rise, partly because the critters have built up resistance to chemicals used previously.

FACT: It's neither here nor there. Lice immediately beget new lice. They produce tons of eggs that hatch, only to feed off the scalp. Getting rid of them takes weeks of concerted effort, special combs and chemical onslaught. Increasing incidence or no, every case is hard to nix. Check out your local drugstore, heavily stocked with anti-lice arsenals. Look on the unpopular bottom shelf, or ask your local teacher or school administrator. Head lice are a fact of life.

UNPROVEN RUMOR: Dirty hair attracts lice more than clean hair.

FACT: Lice infestation has nothing to do with your family's level of hygiene. Like vampires, lice are equal-opportunity bloodsuckers.

Can We Please Change The Subject?

No, we can't. If you're unlucky enough to have to deal with head lice, the time to discover **how** to deal with lice is not when you get the phone call/text/email from daycare or preschool – it's now!

Stages of Grief, As Applied To Lice Warfare

Denial
OMG, this can't be happening! The kids can't miss school! Can't let anyone find out!

Anger
Who's going to babysit the kids AND launder everything in sight AND comb nits AND cook meals? I can't take all that time off from work!

Bargaining

- Maybe if I just spray their heads, slather them in mayonnaise, and cover them with shower caps overnight, or put them in a breathing apparatus for an hour while their heads are fully submerged in underwater, this will just go away?

- I **must** have combed out all the nits, right?

Depression

- I can't face another week of this combing hell without having a major breakdown.

- Dear heaven, I think I just spent all my hard-earned vacation hours... on lice removal.

Acceptance

Damn it, these lice aren't leaving without big-time scissor action – we are having family haircuts STAT. Bald is Beautiful!

Moving On

(We added this Stage because lice sufferers need something loud and empowering.)

NO, YOU CAN'T borrow that hairbrush, bike helmet, ski helmet, or hat. PUT IT DOWN!

Questions About Lice

- Is my family under quarantine? For how long?

- Do I need to put a tent, like a termite tent, over my house? (Having experienced lice removal with his younger sister, our dear friend Lucy's six-year-old pointed to a termite-tented house and calmly stated, "Oh, they must have lice.")

- How long will my kids be out of school?

- What will we do with each other during that time, and how will we avoid killing each other?

- Who is going to comb out Mom?

What you need to do with a lice infestation is to conduct multiple battles involving chemicals, combings, and cleanings, in rapid iteration. After you are fairly certain you have gotten rid of the live lice, your child may return to school.

Sounds simple and fast, right? Bwahhaahahaha!

Your Guide To Lice Combat

PHASE I: Discovery

Symptom
An obvious sign of lice is an itchy head. Similar to symptoms from mosquito bites – feeding off human blood – those afflicted with lice experience itching sensations from lice saliva and open bites. If you notice your child repeatedly scratching his or her head, look for lice.

What Do I Look For?
Lice lay tiny white eggs, the size of dandruff. They stick like glue to strands of hair close to the scalp. You'll read that louse eggs concentrate around the ears, but from what we have seen, eggs appear to be distributed equally around the whole head. Chara confirms this from her experience as a lice checker. In addition, an employee of seven years at a local lice salon, who has combed out louse eggs from thousands of Bay Area heads, reports the same.

Look For White ...
If the nit is a newly laid egg, or leftover shell casing from an already-hatched louse, it is white. So when you spot something that looks white, first determine if it is dandruff, random debris, or an actual nit. Pluck the strand of hair, and wave it around. Dandruff falls off with a flick of your finger. In contrast, a nit will stick to the strand of hair. An egg looks like

a shiny chrysalis upon maturation, but a little speck of dandruff when newly hatched. Are you having fun yet?

... And Look For Shiny Brown

When there is a louse larva developing inside the egg, the nit is a brown color. Therefore, also look for brown eggs. Brown is not as easy to spot in dark hair; but as larvae develop, they have sheen, so look for something shiny.

Do Adult Lice Look Like Bugs?

No, not really. Lice are so small that they look more like specks to the naked eye. Not only are they microscopic, they're also fast and evasive. It's only when you start combing out the affected hair and wiping the comb on a light-colored towel that you will see them. By the way, the lice stick in the comb's teeth, so removal literally goes like this: comb, wipe, comb, wipe, comb, wipe... for hours. With the exception of very fine blond hair, you have to search for nits (not the live bugs) to verify the presence of lice — as the nits don't move.

How Do I Know For Sure That We Have Lice?

If your partner can't find the cinnamon in the spice rack or the milk sitting in the fridge, then don't expect him or her to be able to verify the presence of a microscopic organism on a scalp. If you don't know of a friend or community member experienced with lice, go to a lice salon or ask your school's staff. As a last resort, make a doctor's appointment.

PHASE 2: Attack

Cold, Hard Reality

When you have to get rid of lice, it really is mother-f-ing-emotional-collapse awful. So, we believe the best defense is hardcore offense: think thermonuclear war. This is no time to feel sorry for bugs. Suit up for combings galore, with marathon laundering and chemical bombs a-plenty. Keep combing every day for a week until there are NO LICE OR NITS

LEFT, because you sure as hell don't want to find any nits a few days later and have to start **all over again**.

Lori Burrows Warren on Facebook: "Today's gratitudes:
That my house is fairly small. Makes cleaning easier.
That my dear friend referred me to an amazing local lice removal salon.
That I have an awesome, working washer and dryer. Yep, this is my life this week."

Approach	Minimum	Hardcore
Equipment	• Plastic comb from lice treatment box • Light-colored towel • Bowl of water • Hair clips • Lollipops or bribe food • Vacuum (for house) • Washing machine • Drying machine	Same as **Minimum**, plus ... • Metal comb purchased separately from treatment box • Valium (for you) • Electric lice-zapping comb
Chemicals	Over-the-counter lice removal solutions	Same as **Minimum**, plus ... • Lice-preventative hair conditioners and shampoos such as essential oils and mint • Household lice-killer spray

Approach	Minimum	Hardcore
Process	*Find a really well-lit work area, ideally, outdoors* • Bomb head with chemicals • Comb, endlessly • Vacuum everything • Launder everything that comes in contact with head • Dry items on high heat for 20 minutes	Same as **Minimum**, plus ... • Haircuts for the whole family, including the babysitter and nanny! • Fumigate house

Chemicals Are Your Friend

Use OTC head lice treatments liberally. Regardless of which product you purchase, plan on several boxes per application to cover everyone's hair. Again, we're advocating for the un-PC approach: don't waste your precious time with pacifist homeopathic remedies. We come by our recommendation the hard way: Chara went down an earnest, Cetaphil-laden, tree-hugging route per her doctor's suggestion, only to be utterly defeated by lice. After seven straight days of lotion coatings, dryings and combings, Chara still came upon two adult lice LURKING in her daughter's hair, like Green Berets! At that point, she abandoned her notions of ecologic gentility and went chemical.

Extra Steps For Eliminating Lice

- Use a long metal comb, sold separately, for the most effective solution. Plastic works, but not as well, because the teeth break. Metal will get you there much faster.

- Organize the following supplies in outdoor light or the brightest indoor lighting possible: Comb, cup of water, lice-spray, towel, hair clips, and bribe food.

- Set child in front of a movie or video game.

- Spray hair with lice conditioner to loosen eggs and, ideally, use a product that paralyzes the bugs. Section the hair with clips. Comb out hair, section by section.

- For every stroke of the comb, dip the comb in water, and swipe against the towel to see what goodies you find. Surprise? Surprise! Surprise.

- Every time you conduct a lice treatment, wash and put the following items in the dryer for 20 minutes: car seats, portable car seats, pillows, bedding, hair brushes, hats, jackets, stuffed animals, etc.

- Buy/borrow an electric lice-zapping comb for use on dry hair post-treatment. For Chara, this seemingly desperate step was what finally worked, successfully killing live lice with electrical current. If only she had caved in and spent the money sooner, she would have saved days in the de-lousing process and hours of worry and tiredness.

OR, skip all the tips outlined above, and go straight to a lice salon or paid specialist.

Tell Everybody!

You have lice, and now it's time to blast out the emails. Sure, people might avoid you for a week, but after that, you are in the clear. It's the RIGHT thing to do.

The moment Chara learned her family had head lice, it took 10 years off her life. She had no idea that lice were in her community. She quarantined the house and told NOBODY, not even her BFFs! The mere thought of her kids being the subject of local gossip and spreading lice was mortifying. Amidst this disaster, however, the nanny grapevine kicked in. Through these household helpers, Chara quickly learned of all the families about town who had previously had lice. Well, well, well. No need to move to another state, after all.

Returning to School

It's cool for kids who have been treated to return to school. With the majority of the infestation under control (i.e. the child has had a treatment and is nit-free), the risk of spread is low enough to return to civilization. The endorsement comes with the stipulation that parents are searching and combing daily – both before and after school **for the next several weeks.**

STRAIGHT TALK: Lice Are Everywhere

Don't be embarrassed, and don't delay in calling a professional if there is more than one family member to de-louse.

Not-So-Crazy Tip: Why wouldn't you give your newly-pregnant girlfriend a gift basket that includes some of the usual expectant-mother stuff and also a state-of-the art, electric lice comb? Best $25 ever spent!

Chapter 12

Think You Don't Have Food Allergy Problems? THINK AGAIN.

Quiz: Which of the following foods are good for bringing to the park?

____ Multi-grain chips with sesame seeds

____ Nutella sandwich

____ Cornbread

____ Trail mix

____ Hard boiled eggs with salt & pepper

Answer: None of the above. What?

Allergic Means Nobody Can Freely Eat

Let us explain.

You're a new parent at the park. Your kid's been playing happily for an hour and now is getting hungry. You remembered to bring a trail mix snack – good! Suddenly, you hear another parent shout, "Anna! Get over here NOW!" and see her clutch her child protectively. Anna's parent tells you off about the deathly risk you are posing by bringing nuts to the park, and eventually lobbies schools, the community, various public services, and the restaurant industry to eliminate these allergenic threats. To her, this seemingly banal snack is the equivalent of razor blades in the sandbox or heroin dealers at the jungle gym.

You are stunned, puzzled and embarrassed. Where's the Ebola outbreak? You thought this would be a peaceful day at the park. But instead, you're feeling like an insensitive, under-educated loser for not planning appropriately – for other people's kids.

Let's take a poll. Among a mixed group of fellow parents, how long do you think it would be before you could have a really candid conversation about the twin burdens of life-threatening food allergies: fear and another layer of unasked for work? Parents whose kids don't have allergies aren't looking to be limited or seriously inconvenienced by having to eat like the kids who do. Parents whose kids do have serious food allergies want their kids to be safe, feel normal, and not have to seek special accommodations. They definitely don't want to worry about the risk of their child dying from a measly nut or berry.

Before having kids, we thought food allergies represented more of an intellectual debate, a policy issue. Now, in the thick of the child-raising years, we seriously considered not writing this chapter at all, out of fear of being ostracized and our families physically threatened. Think we're exaggerating? Hang out at the local preschool during a birthday party, and you'll find out.

Tree-nut-free, pea-free, sesame-free, egg-free, dairy-free, lactose-free, wheat-free, gluten-free, strawberry-free, stone-fruit-free... that's a whole lotta free. So why does it feel like deprivation?

Even if your kids under seven years of age don't have food allergies, there is a good chance that you are struggling to get them to eat a decent variety of healthy foods. It's not uncommon for kids to go through food jags where they will only eat one or two things that are portable (i.e. don't need refrigeration or heating) and are halfway healthy. Classic examples: peanut butter, hard-boiled eggs, crackers, pasta. But if you can't serve peanut butter or eggs, and your kid is going through a no-fruit or-veggie and/or-meat phase, you're up the creek. Get into the kitchen, and try to find something lunch-worthy that fits the bill and has some variety. It's surprisingly hard and inconvenient: just one more thing to have to solve. Maybe you even feel resentful! So tell us, what will your kid eat for snack and lunch every day for the next few weeks?

If your kids do have serious food allergies, you're in an even leakier boat. Not only do you have to watch what goes into their mouths, you have to be aware of what's within reach of their little paws. Your new unasked-for life is about limits and inconvenience, coupled with incessant worry. You just want someone to cut you some slack for one friggin' day, so you don't have to think about what ingredients are in that dish. It's quite a burden, and there's no escaping it. Maybe you even feel resentful! Wouldn't it be nice if other parents were supportive and accommodating? Is that so much to ask?

The strain on parents with food-allergic kids goes beyond the health risks. It's painful to watch your child feel different from other kids, because he or she can't eat the birthday cake that contains eggs and gluten. So you end up wishing all of the other school parents would provide treats that meet the lowest common eating denominator.

Here's our feeling, which we think others might share, but are unlikely to utter aloud or otherwise admit. All parents have a cross to bear with their children – this is just one more to add to one's list. It's fine to ask what foods are being served, and request that barrels of peanuts (or strawberries, or eggs) be saved for a different occasion. But your host isn't throwing this party for you, and they aren't running a restaurant. Feed your kid beforehand and monitor them closely.

To hosts who DO accommodate the detailed needs of all of their guests – we applaud you loudly. You're saints. In fact, we kinda wish we had the bandwidth and the household help to pull this off.

To parents like us, i.e. amiable, good-hearted and essentially living the life of slobs who can't get it together, but DAMN IT, we wish we could: we think it's appropriate to communicate what's on the party menu beforehand. Let guests know to bring alternative treats if needed, due to unique or broad-reaching food allergies.

The New Allergy Etiquette is a slippery un-PC slope. Where do the needs stop, and the irrational demands start? Let's examine a range of possible obligations for the following social interactions:

Event: 1:1 playdate at your house

Guest: A child who has serious food allergies

Your Obligation: Full accommodation for your guest

What to Expect from the Parent of the Guest:

Heroic Parent – Brings their own snacks, puts the EpiPen on the kitchen counter, shows you how to use it, and doesn't make a big deal of things. Is alert, calm and competent.

DEFCON 2 Parent – Reviews the contents of your pantry a week in advance, re-shelves your "problem foods" so they are out of reach, and has you initial a form listing approved snack options. Sprays your kid's hands and mouth with disinfectant.

Unmentionable Thoughts: Thank God my kid doesn't have those allergies. How would we get through the day? We're barely treading water as it is. Man, I hope the EpiPen isn't necessary today. Breathe. Breathe. Did she just re-shelve every food item in my kitchen?

Event: Playgroup at home of a child with food allergies

Your Obligation: Bring your usual diaper bag of supplies, including snacks and drinks for the younger siblings, but not anything you know will be a problem. Hope there's enough for everyone.

What to Expect from the Host:

Heroic Host – Provides allergen-free snacks, explains the situation, and asks that anything potentially allergenic that you brought be eaten on the patio with hand washing after. No biggie.

DEFCON 2 Host – Next to the doorbell, there's a red biohazard sign stating "This is an egg-free, wheat-free, nut-free home." The allergic kid is decked out with stickers on chest and back, listing problem foods. When you pop a cracker in younger sibling's mouth (produced in a facility that may have contained nuts), DC2 Host does a head-spinning, foaming-at-the-mouth version of Linda Blair, and everyone runs for their lives.

Unmentionable Thoughts: Um, what is a gluten, does it grow on a tree, or is it alive? Did I just get yelled at in public about a cracker? There were no nuts on it.

Event: Group playdate or party at your house

Your Obligation: Each guest should be able to eat at least one food item without anaphylactic shock entering the picture.

What to Expect from Parent of Kid with Food Allergy:

Heroic Parent – appreciates the fun event and is psyched for their kid to be able to enjoy one food item in common with the group. Brings their own allergen-free treat. Parent is responsible for whatever's ingested.

DEFCON 2 Guest – Calls ahead "to discuss menu" which he or she not-so-subtly edits, lobbying for different foods. Requests that you save all food packaging for ingredient scrutiny. Constantly wipes the table and the hands of all the kids.

Unmentionable Thoughts: Here we go again. I really want to serve frozen pizza. How do I tell the parent that we're having pizza, without feeling like an a-hole?

Event: Birthday at preschool or kindergarten

Your Obligation: Follow the school's policies. For example, classmates are all offered the same event-appropriate treat.

What to Expect from Parent of Kid with Food Allergy:

Heroic Parent – Keeps a stock of allergen-free treats (frozen or packaged) at school for such occasions. Has provided school with EpiPen. Teachers are trained on usage. Carry on!

DEFCON 2 Parent – Emails the entire class at the start of the year, identifying all allergies and outlining specific, acceptable treats, so everyone can eat at the lowest common denominator, even if that means frozen, pureed kale popsicles. Party on.

Unmentionable Thoughts: Have you tasted these everything-free cakes? How do people choke them down? Shouldn't the birthday kid be able to have something other than a kale popsicle?

STRAIGHT TALK

Parents may surprise you. Make sure you understand the extent of the kid's allergy!

- "playing it safe" unwillingness to expose their kids to what could be a potential allergen

- mild sensitivity

- major intolerance

- life-threatening-get-the-EpiPen-and-call-911-NOW.

When a parent says, "Oh, Billy is allergic, so please make sure not to have any nuts during the playdate, wipe down the tables and guarantee that all the kids wash their hands thoroughly before and after eating", ask for the EpiPen and demonstration on usage, get an emergency number for the parent, plus the name and number of their pediatrician, and the preferred hospital should an emergency arise. **This smokes out a lot of the parents for whom food allergies aren't a reality,** but are "avoiding foods that are common allergens until the kids are older." **Parents whose kids have a very real allergic condition** are generally more than happy to provide this information, and usually thrilled to have another adult on top of it.

TIP: If you have kids, you'll be accommodating food allergies from birth through elementary school. Get used to it. Parents are (understandably) rabid about the topic, so even though you don't have time to wipe your own ass these days, have your closest friends give you a list of snacks that their kids can eat and keep a small stash in your house for them.

Chapter 13

The 11th Commandment: Thou Shall Not Call Any Kid "Mean" or "Bully"

Rhymes With Bean, Starts With An M

As a basic adjective, mean, schmean, what's the big deal? We were surprised to learn that it's become unacceptable to describe kids as "mean" – even if the shoe fits. People whisper the word and dance around it. It's easier to say "bossy", "difficult" or "kid drama" – but heaven forbid that a kid should be called mean. Your kid's preschool teacher won't say the word out loud.

We're putting "mean" back into the lexicon. Per Daniel Webster, who published that dictionary in 1825: "Characterized by petty selfish behavior; unkind, unwilling to give or share things; lack of generosity, stingy, offensive; not caring, causing trouble." All kids under three behave like this from time to time and to different degrees. Around ages four to six, kids with consistently nasty intentions start to stand out.

As for "bully" – oh my, no. Let that word fly, and expect a writ from an attorney.

So Mean, So Soon

No kid is an angel, but we were taken aback by just how mean kids can be, and so young. We figured real nastiness came out in the tween or high school years. How naïve we were. We didn't anticipate teaching a preschooler how to deal with a five-year-old who's constantly telling them they can't be in a particular spot because it's Reserved for Someone Else (VIP) at circle time, recess, lunch, and waiting in line for paintbrushes. That's why we're making a point of mentioning it now. Don't be surprised by encounters with Mean kids before the age of six, and some degree of torment from those events. Further, brace yourself for rocky interactions with Mean kid's parents. Remember, their kid is not the one suffering. Au contraire: they may have named it "leadership", "determination" or "decisiveness". Their kid knows exactly what s/he wants and isn't afraid to go for it!

Parental Denial Quiz

Other parents quickly sniff out a Mean kid, but we all have our blind spots with our own children. Maybe you do too. How many of these apply to your kid who is between three and six years old?

- Adjective(s) you use to describe/excuse your child: "sensitive," "socially immature," and/or "high-spirited."
- At home, your child won't relinquish control of toys, lunch chair, or car seat (even if a younger child requires it). Playdates at your house are a regular battle over who can use what and things that are "special."
- When not getting his/her way, your child regularly screams, name calls, has a tantrum, and/or physically harms their playmate.

- Problems or drama break out pretty consistently when your child is playing with siblings or friends at any social event; everyone else has been managing without incident.

- You find yourself explaining often that your child "knows exactly what they want." S/he doesn't go with the flow, from being asked to join a game, taking a turn, or even something as benign as taking a photo.

- Your kid prefers to play with the same one or two kids, often on your kid's terms and makes a point of preventing others from joining play.

- Your kid tells others who not to like, befriend, or play with at preschool.

If you said yes to three or more of these behaviors and don't think of your child as needing attention, you may want to think again. The burden is on YOU to keep the peace and teach reasonable behavior to your child. Nobody said this was easy.

Come Out, Come Out, Wherever You Are

If you're the parent of a Mean kid, i.e. a kid who's been behaving in a Mean way consistently, we recommend that you come out to other parents. Making a clean breast of it can open doors to support, empathy and maybe even a solution. Don't make excuses, don't minimize it, and don't pretend it isn't there, because it's the 9,000-lb gorilla in the room. Your kid's behavior IS your problem. Even if you've tried every bit of advice and nothing's worked; even if you're bone tired and frustrated; even if you've sent your kid to therapists, with and without you – it's still your issue, because you're the parent and the adult.

Better to have it all out in the open and form a village to help: it takes way more than one or two people to correct this behavior in children!

What Kind of Mean-kid Parent Are You?

The Enabler says things like:

- Ashley is very sensitive and really needs to have things her way. (To everyone else, Ashley lacks perspective, gets upset easily, stays upset, and attacks others when upset. She's not so much sensitive as she is insensitive – to others).

- Your kids are not gentle with our little Mitchell's toys. (Grasping to rationalize Mitchell's abhorrent behavior.)

- Our Elliot knows exactly what he wants. He has a "vision" of how he wants to play with others. (Does that mean: if the other kids can't stand the heat, they should get out of the Playskool kitchen?)

The Denier says things like:

- Oh, Cammie, you know we don't push others out of the tree-house, sweetie!

- Now, Harry, we talked about letting others into our car and allowing them to use the carseats during carpool.

- Oh honey, it hurts Mommy's feelings when you yell at me!

- Little Johnny simply gets riled up when he vibes on the negative energy of his peers.

- Kids will be kids!

The Owner says things like:

- Look, Bobby has been a total pill lately, and we have a full discipline plan in place at home. Here are the details. If you see him acting up in school or at your house, please let me know immediately, and feel free to apply the plan, too.

- Oh, I understand why your kid is crying and I am so sorry. We are having a hard time teaching our Joey to share. He will give the item back and apologize. If not, he will be leaving.

- Bella can have a playdate, but I want to limit it to 1½ hours. Please let me know exactly how it went, warts and all. We've been working on her behavior, but she has a ways to go. If she doesn't respect your house or family rules during this playdate, please call.

- Just wanted to check in with you. Have you noticed or heard anything about Lauren's behavior in class or on the playground? We know she has some difficulties, and we want to keep tabs on how she is doing. Thank you so much for your support and help.

It's Not Easy For Any Parent

It's no picnic, living with a difficult, sensitive, high-maintenance, demanding, easily-upset or taken-off-balance, always-in-crisis kid. Children who are hard to handle and chronically misbehave often have parents who have had to lower or change their standards just to be able to cope and keep the relationship with their child intact at home and in a public setting. On the flip side, the rest of us who come into contact with that child and family may not feel the same obligation to make allowances, because we don't have to deal with the behavior day-in and day-out. In the wake of this mess can be hard feelings, hurt feelings, and decisions that sadly make us avoid 1:1 playdates and, in extreme cases, exclude the family entirely.

Although we hope parents in these situations find a way to step out of the daily swirl and regain a little perspective, you'll know the ship has sailed when you hear things like:

- "We parents should stay out of it. The kids will work it out." (In mild cases this works, but serious recurring Meanness requires intentional, consistent, thoughtful intervention.)

- "If your kids are friends with my Mean and continue to attempt a relationship, then your kids must be getting something out of it." (Er, no. Our kids are not getting satisfaction from being manipulated and pushed around.)

- "Well, we **told** Mean that s/he wasn't being nice." (Great! How effective was that?)

Parents – take responsibility! Don't behave as if it's unthinkable to admit that we all need to get our children into line, pronto!

And For Parents of Meanness Recipients

Observing your child being subjected to Mean behavior regularly probably boils your blood or breaks your heart – take your pick. Some options:

- Approach Mean's parent with facts, as calmly and respectfully as you can muster. Although they may not be receptive to the discussion, it's worth a try. Never hurts to be transparent and upfront.

- Teach your kid to stand up for him/herself by role-playing. Find friends and kids who will support your kid openly and in front of Mean kids.

- Have your child express a simple written statement of feelings in I-message form ("I feel __ when you __, because __. Instead I wish __."). Request that a schoolteacher to facilitate direct conversation between the kids.

- Suggest to your kid that s/he build solid relationships with other children. Foster new relationships by offering playdates at your home. Although we realize avoiding the problem kid isn't really practical or sustainable, this is an effort to build support and confidence.

Look, there isn't a "silver bullet" solution, but we believe there's hope for all kids. The more directly the behavior is addressed, the more hopeful we are for a good outcome.

STRAIGHT TALK: Welcome Back To ~~High School~~ Kindergarten!

You thought high school was in your rear-view mirror for good. You moved away from your hometown years ago, built terrific college friendships and enjoyable professional relationships, and put those painful "Heathers" type memories behind you.

Well, sorry to burst your bubble, but when Queen Bees procreate, they like to form power groups to relive their Glory Years. Why leave high school if that's when you peaked? Kindergarten, therefore, is where a new generation of social climbing and power playing formalizes its debut.

Bambi Mom	Queen Bee Mom	Psycho Mom
Enthusiastically signs up for class volunteering each week. One big happy family of parents! Can't wait to meet people and build community.	Excuse me, doesn't do sign-up sheets. (What is this, a democracy?) Crosses off the names of others who signed up in her preferred time slots (for her and her BFF). Someone can tell those Bambi Moms that the spots already were taken.	Distracts teacher, hijacks sign-up sheet, hogs all the Mondays & Fridays, which have the most no-school days. To anyone else who tries to sign up, tells them that Fight Club is coming.
After kinder drop-off, says hello and leaves campus with whoever is around. More community time!	After drop-off, avoids eye contact with Bambis and Psychos by staring at the bulletin board, which hasn't changed in six weeks. Pretend it's faaassincating.	Feverishly apes the QB Moms' thoughtful "contemplating" of bulletin board that's been unchanged for weeks, while (not-so) secretly surveying the social landscape. Then, breaks character and busts out laughing. Walks away satisfied.

Bambi Mom	Queen Bee Mom	Psycho Mom
Throughout the year, offers and accepts playdates with kids' classmates. Group ones are lovely, all are welcome.	Sorry, booked till the end of the year!	Pitches a tent in the QB's front yard. As the mom comes and goes, pops out shouting, "Is now a good time for a playdate?"
Suggests fun after-school, extra-curricular activities via Yahoo groups. Maybe someone else might like to join, and even carpool!	The next 40 months are spoken for, sorry.	Tweets the QB moms' whereabouts & reposts their Facebook check-ins.

Coming To My Birthday?

Birthday parties are a hidden source of sore feelings and angst among parents. Something as seemingly simple and straightforward as a little kid's birthday party can turn into a social weapon. Invitations may have less to do with the kid's actual friends and classmates, and much more to do with parents solidifying desirable social bonds under the guise of "Hey, my kid is turning five!"

To address the problem of social exclusion, some preschools and schools require parents either to include all the boys, all the girls, or the entire class. Imagine a dozen girls and boys each. In kindergarten, the class is an extended family of sorts, and parents are feeling united. That is, until the birthday invitations and FB celebration photos come out. Suddenly, you realize Bobby invited only some of the other (toddler) boys in his class to his birthday ... and not yours. Wow. Who knew this was part of preschool learning? Tempting as it may be to reciprocate the no-invite when your own kid's birthday rolls around, we know you will take the high road. Consider the following birthday etiquette for at least the initial years of elementary school:

- Invite all boys and/or all girls in the classroom.

- If you have a neighbor with the same age child in the school, invite them as well, if your party will be right in their face or over the fence.

- Consider joint parties with other kids who were born in the same month or quarter and invite the class. Frankly, at this age, they barely notice. Put a little cake in front of them, a few balloons and a jumpy house, and they're golden. It also takes away the pressure to work around other parents' party dates. Many private and co-op schools encourage and coordinate joint parties. Think of the money you will save, and you can still have a family or private celebration at home.

- Party favors – after many years of disposing of cheap plastic toys that end up in the garbage and then landfill, we say ease off on party favors! If you can't stand the thought of not having favors, consider a gift swap, a book exchange or a contribution to a charity.

- "No Gifts Please" – It's your call. Gifts make a very special day, and it adds to the fun for your kid. It also is ritualistic – children like to wrap, decorate, and carry gifts to the party to mark the occasion. When the kids are very young, keep gifts to around $10, and focus on having fun together. Books are a great gift; check Daedalus Books & Music online for Caldecott and Newbery award winning titles in hardback and paperback, at remainder prices.

TIP: Birthday parties are all about excitement and the creation of fond memories for your child and those that attend. Sometimes homespun parties are the most warm, fuzzy and all-out fun. They absolutely, positively DO NOT have to cost a lot of money, nor do they require artistic talent. However, they usually do require letting others help, and delegating, delegating, delegating. Have aunts/uncles, grandparents or friends pitch in to run Musical Chairs, Pin the Tail on the Donkey, water balloon tosses (seriously awesome), Piñata (with pennies, stickers, etc.) and so on. Turn on music and the bubble machine for a "Freeze" strike-a-pose-dance-a-thon. Have a shaving-cream party with the kids in bathing suits outdoors – let them decorate their faces, hair, tummies, whatever! Schedule the party during a snack time with simple finger foods: popcorn, watermelon, snap peas, drinks and cupcakes displayed on the table for all to self-serve. K.I.S.S. Put a bottle of wine, crudites and dip on the table for parents who would like to stay!

Chapter 14

Bringing It Home

O ver the years, we've been made to feel that if we talk openly about how rough things are, it's as though we are being un-American. There is sympathy for those pulling themselves up by their bootstraps, putting themselves through school, going through rehab, or trying to find work. But nowadays, parenting little ones is treated like a religion – as though it should be a cause for worship and a constant source of exaltation. Huh? We're sorry, but child adoration doesn't do the laundry, schedule the appointments, puree the vegetables, change the diapers or do the chauffeuring. The smell of the baby's hair doesn't balance the checkbook, pay for daycare, help you figure out how to stay awake even though you've been up the last 4 nights dealing with bedwetting, or address the fact that you and your partner are too tired and discouraged to connect much.

So we wrote this book to release parents of children under seven from the self-imposed guilt and stress of thinking:

- parenting little kids should be straightforward, if not easy
- everyone else has it figured out
- since I don't have it all figured out, I must be a loser, and
- what's more, I must be a terrible parent

While we can't offer a miracle to fix all your parenting difficulties, we can bring this conversation down to earth and **into the open**. Now that we have, here is what we're asking you to do:

1   Be real. No need to pretend that it's easy. It's okay to say to people that you're having a hard time. This is not whining: it's a statement of fact.

2   Let others take care of your kid, and let them do it their way, as long as safety is not an issue. You need the break.

3   Form playgroups and get together regularly instead of paying for "baby enrichment" classes. Seek playgroups with like-minded individuals. Hint: if you feel like you have to be "on," it's not the right playgroup for you!

4   Change a few habits to make things easier for yourself. In a pinch:

   - Let the kids watch TV for a bit, even it it's horrible programming.

   - Oatmeal is perfectly fine for dinner.

   - Take a shower, even if your kid cries (or screams) because you're not paying attention to him or her for 15 minutes. Make sure said child is safe first – crib, playpen, etc.

5   At the end of the day, here are the things we wish we had let go of sooner:

   - Feeding only "super foods"

   - 100% home-cooked meals

   - Letting others change the diaper, feed a bottle, dress the toddler, put him/her down for a nap, and give the bath.

   - Obsessing over early achievement of baby/toddler milestones

   - Stressing out over baby/toddler second language immersion

- So many pointless enrichment classes
- Wearing a jacket when it's cold outside, wearing PJs to bed, wearing "proper clothes" instead of anything that's almost clean

6   Find confidantes so you can vent, get perspective and problem-solve career and family issues alike. Preferably, in your playgroups. You'll need objective yet supportive voices from those in a similar boat, cheering you on. With them, you won't have to bear the burden of pretending that everything's great, either.

This book is our validation to you: parenting's gotten really difficult, and we are *all* struggling! And know this: it will take a while, but you'll eventually rebound and slowly reclaim your life.

Our Final Top Ten, Just For You

What They'll Say	What They Should Be Saying
You're having a baby! Congrats! How wonderful!	You're having a baby? Hope you have $1.5 M socked away in solid income-producing investments. Here's $25 to get you started!
You're expecting? No wonder you're glowing! Your hair is just gorgeous!	From now until you deliver, indulge in 20-minute showers, do the full hair-and-makeup routine, and take as much time as possible! Memorize this feeling and take note of the results. It'll need to last you for six years.
I bet you're looking forward to starting a family! Baby makes three!	Yes, baby makes three. Nonetheless, pay attention to yourself, the state of your marriage or partnership, and your baby – in equal measure. Raising a kid from age 0 – 5 takes a village and one person does not make a village.
Have you picked out your baby announcements? Got them all ready for your partner to mail out on the big day?	Have you researched all the preschools? Scheduled the pre-interviews? Filled out the applications? Worked your social network to give you a leg up toward admission?

What They'll Say	What They Should Be Saying
What color did you pick out for the nursery? Matching toy baskets and liners?	What calendar system did you choose, to manage the family schedule of activities and drop-off/pick up responsibilities? Do you have auto-pay set-up?
Are you considering a doula and natural childbirth, or are you going for the epidural?	Are you considering a part-time sitter, having a cadre of mother's helpers, or are you going for the live-in au pair?
Do you know if it's going to be a boy or a girl? Picked any names yet?	Do you know how to cook nut-free, dairy-free, gluten-free, kid-friendly meals and snacks?
How long are you taking for maternity leave? Looking forward to relaxing and bonding with the baby?	When was the last time you had two full-time jobs? That was pretty relaxing, huh? Bet you didn't realize the office would feel like a vacation compared to managing a toddler and a baby all day and all night.
OMG! Where are you registered?	OMG! If I gift you with a deluxe lice removal kit, will you get freaked out?"
Is your MIL going to stay with the toddler when you're in the hospital delivering?	Are you going to have your regular babysitter or nanny take care of your toddler 24/7, as your MIL's "boundaries" don't allow for cooking, bathing, diaper-changing and/or putting down for naps?

Chapter 15

Tips

Parent Socializing & Support

Make a rest plan, and find a way to get some

When you are a new parent home from the hospital with your new baby, it is totally normal to be worried about his or her breathing, temperature, and comfort. You keep yourself awake, concerned, checking, thinking, and over-thinking. Before you work yourself into an illogical state, maybe sit down and agree to something practical, such as an observation schedule every 4 hours. By the time you have your second child, know that you won't waste a second worrying about this.

Make a nursing plan, and be prepared for it NOT TO WORK

Absolutely, spend some time thinking about your breastfeeding goals. Just know that the best-laid plans go by the roadside, even those crafted by super-planner you. Your baby and your breasts are going to call the shots, not your brain. Latching, positioning, milk production, your baby's preferences – they can't be predicted. Do your best with the hand you've been dealt – your little one, your nipples, your milk glands and mastitis are all in play. Many have a hard time weaning and continue breastfeeding well beyond their expectations. Conversely, others experience complications and discontinue nursing much earlier than they hoped. Our point is that what you want and what actually happens are two different things.

Organize or join a weekly playgroup

Don't be shy. Get the names, numbers, and email addresses of the parents you met at the park whose kids are born within six months of yours. The people who become playgroup stalwarts will be incredibly close friends. They will live with you through kid not sleeping through the night, teething, refusing all manner of foods, vomiting ad hoc for no apparent reason, allergic to whatever, refusing to potty train (#1 and/or #2), becoming hysterical at daily drop-offs, catching every possible germ at daycare and thus requiring second (expensive and stressful) nanny to backfill while unable to go to daycare. These people will be your lifeline. They will bring you meals for WEEKS after you have your second kid and help when you think your life is completely over because the new baby won't latch, you have mastitis, you're hormonal and crying, you're sleepless (forgot that newborns don't sleep, eh?) and your toddler is hating on you. *These are about the only people you will be able interact with, given your postpartum belly, unwashed hair, and schizophrenic mindset.*

Household help

You have no cycles to fully train and deal with your new household help, and so you hope everything will get done, just the way you would do it. Well, plan on that not happening. The golden rule is 80-20. Anything you delegate will get done about 80% right, and the remaining 20% is yours to do the way you want it. Every time you feel frustrated, remind yourself of this rule. There is no escaping it, sister, so accept and own your 20%, no matter how much you pay or how many hours of help you have.

Dining out with kids

Take advantage of places that allow pre-orders by phone. That way, nobody suffers the full agonizing interval between arriving at restaurant and actual plates of food hitting the table. Bring something for kids to do – crayons, silly putty, finger puppets, board books, small blocks and a couple of big plastic cups – while waiting as little as possible for service or food. Keep a drawstring bag of this stuff in your car for grab/go.

Babysitting

If you meet a responsible teen/tween who is interested in babysitting, limit the stint to 2-ish hours. Seldom, short and fun is the name of the adolescent sitter game; even if they say they can handle longer time periods. In affluent towns, the tweens don't need the money either. So what you have to do is find as many responsible babysitters as you can, and rotate them.

Be sure to check out your local YMCA – they offer very affordable child-care at their facilities. Perfect opportunity for a workout!

Go easy on yourself, and be careful with those "When I'm A Parent" fantasies

The media makes it seem like every moment with your child should be filled with joy and sunlight, Hallmark memories, retouched Instagram selfies, and an Oscar-worthy soundtrack as accompaniment. Hmmm. It's more normal to be bone tired much of the time. It's also normal to be feeling defeated pretty regularly. Whether it's the baby not spending tummy time without crying, eating solids by such and such a month, sleeping through the night regularly or walking by X months, the opportunities for concerns are endless. Keep in mind that progress often looks like 2 steps forward, 1 step backward. When things are not panning out the way you wanted or planned, it doesn't automatically mean everything is going to hell in a hand-basket. It means there is a gap between your expectations and the present reality. Let go of expectations grounded in mass media fantasy or "expert" opinion in the blogsphere. Every child is different. Discuss with your pediatrician.

Strange But Oh-So-True

Does that diaper really need changing?

When was the last time you wore a diaper? You might be surprised how their technology has improved. Diapers really never feel that wet at all, and might NOT be the source of your child's crying. On her second child, Chara used a fraction of the diapers lavished on her first. Why? Well, as her first always cried, she changed the diaper in case that was the possible cause. By her second child, she realized she had previously been changing what was in fact a "moist" puffed-up diaper containing sweat, not urine. Moreover, Chara learned that she just didn't need to be so obsessed about it. Helen used a hairdryer (set on low) during diaper changes, because her eldest hated cold air on his butt. As a second-time mom, she was absolutely deaf to such complaints.

I like to use the toilet by myself, thanks

When the kids are 0-6, it's rare they'll let you alone long enough for you to sit on the toilet. So expect your kid to stand by while you take a dump. Oh, and they're more than likely close enough to practically sit on the toilet with you, and often will. If you can manage to close the door before they barge in, they'll happily talk through it, asking questions and wanting to show you what they're working on. We can honestly share that we've not had a private toilet moment in our own homes in five years.

Birthday suit

Chara felt embarrassed when her toddler would get herself naked and run around the house, down the street or at the park with water features, ever so happy in her birthday suit. NOT open to putting her clothes back on. The Germans at the park said to her, "All the little kids run naked in Germany, at least until age seven!" and, therefore, Chara almost exclusively hung out with German folk over the next year. Our vote is that two-year-olds can be appropriately naked in the outdoor family play setting including the beach, park, front yard and neighborhood. Can't they be uninhibited for a nanosecond of their lives? Really, people, find something else to bitch about.

We're Parents, Let's Stick Together

Pre-meal snacks within a half hour of mealtime
YES to fruits, veggies, cheese, small amount of whole-grain healthful items. NO to candy, soda, processed food "fillers," and bowls of Goldfish/Chex Mix, including at birthday parties and playdates when just before lunch or dinner.

Public peeing in a bush during potty training
We say YES to being tolerant and cool, when the kid is in early phases of potty training. Ages two to three get a pass to use nature in obscure places if a bathroom isn't accessible. Just be as considerate as possible, going to the farthest bush or tree possible, staying out of public thoroughfares, and best yet bring an empty cup you can then dispose in the trash. We say NO to prissy people who are rigid about the outdoors. How much liquid volume can a two-year-old's bladder hold, anyway?

The Tooth Fairy
YES to a cool 50-cent piece or a Susan B. Anthony dollar coin. NO to a $20, a $50, or a $100. Or a Tesla.

Allowance
YES when limited to the child's grade (in dollars) per month for acceptable behavior and expected contributions to the household. NO to a Jay-Z style budget for the toddler. To what end?

You, Personally

Lanolin
Do not underestimate the use of lanolin. The moment your nipples become chapped, you are DONE. Apply 24/7 before it is too late.

Hair maintenance
Welcome to the brave new world of dry shampoo/wash sprays that literally de-grease your hair. You will learn to appreciate these sprays sold at drug stores and hair salons, because they will be your ONLY option for the many times you just can't pull yourself together, but also can't look like a street urchin. Not kidding.

Slip-on footwear
As absurd as this sounds, you will eventually purchase boots and shoes based on whether you can slip them on and off without having to bend down. No consideration for style. Much like Moms in Mom Jeans, now it's Moms in Mom Shoes. Because the simple act of bending and tying a boot or shoe with a sleeping baby in your arms feels like a straw-breaking moment.

Books that mattered
In addition to the usual from Brazelton, the American Academy of Pediatrics, et al:

1-2-3 Magic, Thomas W. Phelan

How to Talk So Kids Will Listen & Listen So Kids Will Talk, Adele Faber & Elaine Mazlish

Siblings Without Rivalry, Adele Faber & Elaine Mazlish

Between Parent and Child, Haim C. Ginott

Why Gender Matters, Leonard Sax

The Female Brain, Louann Brizendine

Maybe Baby, Lori Leibovich (ed.)

Random Time-Savers

Program pediatrician info into partner's phone

Line up your pediatrician a few months before the baby is due. (We've had the suggestion of choosing the same gender pediatrician as your child, so when they hit puberty they can comfortably ask questions.) On that same day, add the doctor's full contact information into your partner's phone, and tag under "Favorites." Trust us, the last thing you need in the middle of the night while you are falling to pieces consumed with consoling a child, drawing the bath, and cleaning up vomit, is a clueless partner who CAN'T DIAL URGENT CARE.

Customized gift stickers

You won't always have time for a homemade card, so we suggest customized stickers, such as a frog logo with "Hoppy Birthday! From Matthew Smith" that sticks onto gifts or bags. It's a thoughtful move for the receiving parents without loose cards floating about in preparation for the mass of thank-you notes.

Also, an individual or group email "thank you" is perfectly fine. While we were raised to handwrite notes on personal stationery, technology is a fact of life and parents are much busier. We think the intent and overall goal is more important than the actual letterpress and fountain pen method. Some of you will disagree, which is totally cool as well.

Pre-pack those activity bags

This goes for the swim bag, diaper bag, preschool bag, soccer bag, park bag, etc. – keep them stocked and ready at all times. Everyone in the house should learn about where these bags are stored, what goes in them, and most important, returning items straight back to the bags after use. No halfway points. It's too common to find yourself pulling your hair out, searching the laundry room or playroom, running late because you can't locate that One Item.

Household Items

Hellooo, java

Get a coffee maker with an automatic brew setting. Program it every night so it makes coffee without fail at o-dark-hundred. This is the magic that allows you to mobilize the troops for breakfast, pack lunch, get school stuff into bags, shoes on feet, jackets on bodies, strap everyone into the damn car seats, and get out the door into traffic to get the kids to pre-school, so you can get to the office on time. If there is one thing you do every night, setting the coffee maker is IT.

Stemless wine glasses

We can't tell you how many wine glasses have bitten the dust with toddlers around. Stemless glasses have a lower center of gravity and easily fit in the dishwasher. Save the crystal long-stemmed glasses for grown-up tabletop occasions. And when the kids are in the grabby-clumsy-can't-be-reasoned-with stage, take out a bunch of plastic cups and drink from those. You know, the kind you used to have at college keggers. Nobody cares! Your friends are so psyched just to have some ETOH in their system, they're not gonna notice!

Food containers with the same size lid (in bulk)

Keeping an inventory of different containers all with different matching lids chews up time and makes you frustrated. When buying containers of different sizes, choose ones that have the same size lid. No more hunting for the lid to that ONE container. Better yet, if you lose or break the lid, you can still keep the container.

Ditto for sippy cups

See containers above. Don't waste time sorting and matching lids to sippy cups every day.

Vinyl

The hardware store has huge rolls of colored and clear vinyl that can be cut at different lengths. Buy some for the floor under your dining table, over the craft table, wooden train table, and any surface that needs to last for more than three months. The vinyl sheets prevent liquid, paint, markings, and scrapes. We love how PB Kids looks, but it isn't cheap! Vinyl costs $5.00 and will extend the life of your furniture immeasurably. Plus, you won't be freaking out over every little spill.

Holiday décor

Even if you manage to ignore Martha Stewart, you will buckle under your kids' pressure to decorate for the holidays. Irrespective of your native culture and religious beliefs, prepare to have to celebrate Halloween, Thanksgiving, Christmas, Hanukkah, Valentine's Day, St. Patrick's Day, Easter, and Independence Day. When they're little, the kids will be bummed if you don't get spirited for these occasions. Prepare now to buy the minimum look three or more weeks after the holiday has passed, thus saving 75%!

Kids' non-breakable holiday décor

Your Norman Rockwell-style, family Christmas tree decorating vision may literally and figuratively come crashing down without this tip: **buy and store non-breakable ornaments together in a single box designated for the kids.** Don't lessen the joy and excitement by saying "no" and "stop, put that down" hundreds of times. Hand over the box of non-breakables and allow freedom to experiment with hanging ornaments. Hang them at the bottom of the tree, knowing anything within reach will get yanked.

Tip: To keep the tree from tilting or falling amidst toddler activity, place a fish-eye screw at the top of your window molding. Loop fishing wire around the tree, and tie back.

Kid Food

Healthy food

Generally speaking, offer your child a variety of healthy foods. With that said, we advise against being perpetually at war with your kids about their diet. When you're trying to determine if your child has been eating healthfully, we believe in the concept of looking at a week's worth of food intake. Getting stressed out over a day's worth of meals is just not realistic or productive. Read *Crunch A Color* by Jennifer Tyler Lee for a great approach and advice with slightly older kids.

Avoid nuts in public settings

Although you are not personally responsible for other's children, the presence of nuts can be counted on to cause distress. Avoid nut products when in public. Wash your kids' hands and faces after they eat nut products.

Frozen veggies

Many toddlers find chopped frozen vegetable gems (such as a medley of carrots, peas, green beans and lima beans) incredibly enjoyable to eat frozen or slightly thawed. Buy frozen vegetables and pour directly from the freezer into a snack cup. No heating required!

Corn

Microwave corn on the cob with FULL husk on for 1-2 minutes. Don't judge it until you try it. It is fast, easy (no dishes!), and tastes even better than traditional methods. It also tastes great at room temperature, so you can pack it as a snack. Your child only needs two upper teeth – Chara's kids were eating corn straight from the cob as babies. It keeps them busy for a long time ☺. Bonus all around.

So-called popcorn

When the kids are hungry and you are about to start cooking dinner, consider the healthful snack of oven-baked chopped cauliflower, called popcorn. Cut it up, shake it in a bag with olive oil and salt, and cook for 15 minutes at 375 degrees. Much like popcorn, it's crunchy, tasty, and fun!

Sausage

Odds are you'll be cooking sausage of all kinds. Because your kid, if he or she is anything like all the ones we know, will go through a multi-year phase of only eating hot dogs or hot-dog-like substitutes. It will boggle your mind. Learn to deglaze: place uncooked sausage in a shallow pan with ¼ inch of water. After the water fully evaporates and the fat adheres to the pan, add a touch of hot water. Cook until sausage is fully browned.

Kid Clothing

Buy clothes off-season

Save money and buy items when they are off-season. Think ahead, estimate sizes, and buy everything adjustable on clearance. Some off-season clothing basics include winter footie pajamas, jackets, parkas, rain boots, and of course, all things fleece.

Fleece

If they make it in fleece, you're golden. It's washable, expels most stains, doesn't shrink or fade, and BEST OF ALL, retains its thermal properties even when wet! FLEECE! Perfect wear for rainy days, cold beach, and doesn't need to be placed in the dryer after washing. Why don't they make fleece underwear, we want to know?

Clothing with adjustable waistbands

Only buy clothes that have a built-in interior button/elastic system. Avoid faux "drawstrings" that barely work or are sewn onto the exterior for show. You'll get many more months, even years, of wear out of the adjustables.

Buy the same socks in bulk

Socks. Missing socks. Don't bother searching and matching. Who has that kind of time? Instead, buy them all in the same kind/color. For kids who are sensitive to stitching, there are seamless socks (one small stitch at toe line) made of stretchy, lighter material. Because of their elasticity, these socks fit a span of several foot sizes and can be shared among siblings. They also don't retain water/sweat – altogether brilliant. See SmartKnit.com.

Kid Bedroom

Clock + thermometer + white noise machine

Buy an electronic device that triples as an indoor thermometer and plays white noise of ocean waves or other natural sounds. The time and air temperature are illuminated, so you're not constantly second-guessing if the baby's room is too hot or cold. Plus you just can't have enough white noise to preserve your child's sleep. Helen used a CD of beach sounds – even simpler – which both of her kids loved.

Clock with traditional hour/minute hands

Look for a classic clock with traditional hands that illuminate in the dark and ticks relatively quietly. Keep it right next to your digital clock (mentioned above), as an aid to your child learning to tell time. Better yet, tape a piece of paper at the base of the clock that shows the time your kids may leave their rooms after they wake.

Ventilation fan

Use a stand-alone ventilation fan, such as a Honeywell, on a dresser and say goodbye to a stale room reminiscent of your college dormitory. Say hello to the constant lull of the fan's white noise, which helps kids fall and stay asleep. Heaven.

Kid Training

- When your kid says, "I'm not good at it," add the word "YET," to encourage practice. Telling them to keep trying creates the possibility, while acknowledging current conditions.

- When offering treats or special snacks to kids, have one of the kids pass out the food and divvy up to foster sharing.

- Use charts, stars, and carrots for good behavior. New approaches start off with a bang, then begin to lose their luster, so don't be disappointed or surprised: think ahead to your next idea. All you really need is for each new tactic to work long enough to break the cycle of a specific behavior.

- Ask your kids to choose clothes and lunch preferences the **night before**. Don't hesitate to put kids to bed in their school clothes for tomorrow. What the heck – they can't spill food on their clothes while they're asleep. Less laundry, and it saves morning time/drama getting dressed while you are trying to move everyone out the door. It's especially handy when you have to get to work, or if you have a five-year-old or kindergartner who can't be late.

- Draw a smiley face with a marker, one on each of the insides of the sole of your toddler's shoes. Teach them the faces will "kiss" when they put on the correct shoe. Or place a dot where the big toes go.

Kid Management

- Before giving birth to your second child, set aside a basket of "special" items for your older child that ONLY are to be brought out while you are nursing. The hope is that this will keep the first child excited and occupied enough to offset feelings of neglect while you tend to the newborn.

- Just when you feel your patience is at its limit (for example, Day 30 of not getting your kids to cooperate with the bedtime routine), do something funny and unexpected. Helen once made her belly button talk, and to this day, doing it breaks up the tension.

Alternatively, state your child's age out loud to regain perspective – these are wee folk. Or pretend you are Kramer on *Seinfeld*: say loudly, "I NEED A HUG!" Even if it doesn't improve the children's attitude, there is a chance that it will help yours.

- To eliminate badgering by the kids, make a routine out of anything you can. For instance, one dad came up with the slogan, "a quarter after we order" at restaurants with coin game machines. Thus, he doesn't go through the entire negotiation every time. No one says a word, knowing quarters will be handed out after they order.

- By all means, live guilt-free watching TV. Yes, it's super trendy to say that your kids don't watch TV, because it causes brain cell death and they'll never get into Harvard if you let them. The kids could be out splitting the atom instead, and getting published! We're not here to argue the relative merits and problems related to TV-watching. But when we meet a parent who makes these 100% no-TV claims, we think, "BULLSHIT." Pretty much. This is the same family that has a secret *"Real Housewives"* watcher, whose kids are addicted to iPhones and iPads, just you wait. Do yourself a favor. Don't be intimidated by the thought of Perfect Parent whose kids are in Portuguese Immersion all day. Instead, record lots of good shows and movies to play while you take a shower, or grab a badly needed extra half hour of sleep at 5:00 am because your kid is wide awake but you're run ragged. We're not going to judge you, even if we are the ONLY ones not judging you.

Kid Toys, Gear & Activities

Everything gently used

Our watchword: gently used kid items at fraction of the price. New just doesn't matter – everything you buy looks equally tired after three months. Plus, you must save for their college and grad school, remember? Look to your mother's club for this kind of gear exchange. Many of them have some form of classified ads where used strollers, bouncers, baby carriers, high chairs, bikes etc. are traded, bought and sold for very reasonable prices.

Keep that receipt
You can't predict which contraption your three-month-old child will enjoy enough to actually use. Your older one might have loved that side-swinging musical chair, but your younger one absolutely loathes it. Plan to swap, borrow and test items for a few days. Keep trying until you find one that works. Don't worry, your baby will make his or her preferences shriekingly clear. Save the box and all the packaging, because you might be returning it soon or passing it along.

Enhancement/advancement courses for kids under seven
After personally registering her under five-year-old for ice-skating, Spanish, and piano, Chara can tell you emphatically that it made no impact. Sure, it was a fun way to burn an hour, but the fact Skylar had eight private skating lessons costing $400 did NOT, repeat did NOT, create a baseline advantage. By age seven, her ice-skating and Spanish abilities were the equivalent to never having had a lesson at all! If you do it, the reason should be fun and enjoyment, but don't expect it to make a big difference, unless they stick with it weekly for years, practicing for hours.

Toys that were surprisingly worth it
- Scooter with two small wheels in front: As early as 16 months, some kids can work a scooter containing two small wheels in the front and one in the back. Our kids practiced inside the house (the rubber wheels did not affect the floor), and then moved to the sidewalks. Get the *Micro-mini*. The knock-offs don't work as well.

- Professional, electric bubble-making machine: works wonders when you have little guests, and creates a festive environment for all. Helen's alternative: the Joan Crawford Special – a wire hanger bent into a hoop, dipped in a bucket of dish-soap water with a bit of glycerin. Wave it around for humongous bubbles.

- Synthesizer/electronic keyboard: Our kids have been using ours for 8+ years! Again, get a really good one. Put it on the floor and get a microphone or two.

- Roller coaster: If you have a long driveway, it is perfect for a toy called the roller coaster, which is basically a ramp with buggie cart. We are familiar with the ones made by Step 2. They last forever, and when the kids get older, they use the same ramp for their scooters and skateboards. It is costly, but worth it— and we suggest the steepest one.

- Pedal-free bike: The best route to teaching a child how to ride a bike is to start with a pedal-free bike. The kids will scoot around for a few months, and before you know it coasting and balancing with their feet up. The balancing part works best on downhill grades. The days of parents with thrown out backs, and kids with huge bloody knees are over. Borrow this, or look for it used.

- Plasmacar: These pedal-free-scooter-carts work at a very early age both inside and outside the house. Be it a 10-month-old sitting up and getting pushed about, two toddlers sitting together with one steering and the other scooting, or older kids tying it to a bike and hauling each other around... this a winning contraption.

- *Lady Bug* board game: Chara played this board game all the time with the toddlers. Fun, easy to understand and stays fresh/interesting to play with a number of kids.

- *Uno* card game: Not hard to learn, repeat fun for most ages.

- Playing card holder: With this plastic rack (primarily meant for the elderly/arthritic), your toddler can effectively participate with the family in *Uno*, *Old Maid*, and other basic card games. Without the cardholder, it's just not possible for young kids to coordinate holding and managing the deck.

- Bass drum: The very large handmade-leather-bass drums, sturdy enough for little ones to climb onto and large enough for four to six adults and kids alike to comfortably hang around and create rhythm. Large buckets turned upside down work really well too.

Toys & gear that you don't (necessarily) need

High chair
Chara skipped the high chair. Yup, both she and her friend Lillie just used the kind you hitch to a table, or the ones you place on the countertop, chair or her handy-dandy portable baby walker (see tip below). If you don't have kitchen space that goes along with a massive high chair, it's just not a big deal. Once kid is able to prop him or herself up, you can evolve straight to a tiny table and chair ensemble you'll use forever. On the flip side, Helen swore by the high chair, even took it camping! To each her own.

Crib and bassinet
Imagine all the money saved when lightening up the baby registry ☺. Rather than a bassinet, Helen used a baby bathtub placed in a butterfly chair and parked it in her bedroom for a few months. When her son outgrew the bathtub, he moved to a crib, which she found on *Craigslist* unused and in its original packaging from Italy. The sellers discovered that they preferred to have their child co-sleep in their bed. Chara started off using the bassinet attachment of her stroller parked in her bedroom. Then, despite having an assembled crib, her preferred method was to co-sleep with the baby on a mattress (no box spring), placed directly on the carpeted floor, in a corner with a safety bar or swim noodle under the fitted mattress sheet. For Chara, it was way easier to lie down, nurse the baby, then sneak off when baby fell asleep (or nap together).

The point is, don't get suckered into the baby industry and all things that you "have to have." It is A-OK to be resourceful, such as simply using a Pack-n-Play as your crib. Why buy both?

Diaper Genie
Thumbs DOWN to storing several days' worth of diapers in your house. Move 'em out each day. Diapers with #2 should go directly inside a plastic bag knotted and into the outdoor receptacle. Yes, this Diaper Genie is

compact and suppresses odors, but you still have to change out the bags. These are special liners, and they aren't cheap! It's a little like getting sucked into buying that fancy laser printer – the price is right, until you realize the perpetual need for exorbitantly expensive toner cartridges.

Changing station

Helen and Chara put a diaper-changing pad on top of a regular dresser. However, both most often used a foldable/portable changing pad placed wherever, including the floor, bed, couch, etc. The car trunk is in fact the BEST makeshift changing area as it is wind-protected, private, inescapable, and muffles screams of protest. Truth be told, once the child can stand, even if only by propping themselves up, it is preferable to change the diaper right then and there while they are upright, lickety-split. Unless you have a crowd of onlookers, no need to carry a wiggling, kicking, poop-smushed-all-over-the-butt child to a changing station – when you can easily bring the wipes and new diaper to them. BTW, when your child poops to the point of it going up and outside the top of the diaper, it's time to trade up a diaper size.

Bottles

Refusing the bottle around 3+ months old can be normal. It may not be the bottle, the formula, the nipple, or the temperature. If you have a kid who is utterly determined not to drink from the bottle ever again (like both of Chara's kids), try using sippy cups with no valves, or jerry-rig by punching a hole through those soft plastic tops to increase flow. Tiny plastic cups, such as a mouthwash cup, worked for her between breast milk and solids. This was a great lesson learned too late, as Chara spent a great deal of time and money purchasing every bottle, nipple and pacifier known to mankind. Nothing worked – including the paid professional specialist.

When using bottles and nipples, think hot soapy water and not necessarily sterile-field and chemical decontamination. If breastfeeding works, you might bypass bottles altogether. Since neither of her kids would accept a bottle, Chara's husband had to show up at her workplace every three hours with infant so she could nurse. Eventually, her kids migrated sipping two ounces of formula from a small plastic Dixie-like cup.

Baby walker (a retro Yes!)

Call Chara a renegade, but remember those retro baby walking seats? They look like a very low high chair, including tray and wheels. **Don't use it near stairs**. Chara's daughter mostly cried unless she was free to zoom in one. It was perfect for eating, practicing to stand safely, and easily portable... what's not to love? Chara got it for free on the curb! Both children used it religiously. Her first child walked at 13 months and her second walked at nine months.

Car & Home

Car wash and detail

Add "interior car detailing" to your bi-annual, must-do list. For less money then you think, your vehicle will be scraped, scrubbed, and suctioned clean. The detailer will peel the kid-inflicted stickers off your windows, and high-pressure air jets will blast away crumbs and gunk from minute crevices. Even if you are a champion cleaner, you won't be able to match this level of restoration, so don't overlook this opportunity to get back in the Dept. of Health's good graces.

Before the detailing, remove the car seats completely, and hold your breath – otherwise, the odor might knock you out. Seriously, you have no idea how much formula, milk, juice, turkey, cheese and yogurt have fallen in the seat crevices and beneath the car seat fabric. You might observe bugs living off the food hiding between the seatbelt anchors. Sorry to gross you out, but this is based on actual experience. Get your car detailed by a professional.

Carpooling

When buying your family car, figure out how many actual five-point harness car seats fit in the passenger area. If you can't fit more than two (not uncommon), think again. In fact, if you can't get at least four, no chance of anyone carpooling to outings with you, which results in double the gas, double the parking, none of the bonding, and half the fun. This explains the crazy prevalence of the Honda Odyssey and Toyota Sienna.

House remodel

Typically, as your family extends, so does your home out of necessity. Below is our advice regarding home remodeling:

- Get a mobile HVAC unit, one that you can put inside the baby's room to regulate the temperature. If you have to use a hardwired device, be very smart about where this is placed, so it reads a temperature that is similar to that of the bedrooms behind closed doors.

- Place extra insulation (which requires a few more inches in the technical drawings) in between bedroom walls and floors. In fact, we suggest extra insulation all the way around – even for the exterior walls.

- Multiple showerheads and detachable showerheads are helpful.

- Large bathtubs, as typically parents just go in the tub with infants and toddlers.

- Pedal for the sink to turn the water on and off, perfect for when you have goop and potential salmonella on your hands. There is a period when your kids can just reach their hands under the faucet, and it saves water you can continuously control the force with your foot while your hands are busy.

Infant Years

Hospital notables

- Bring wipes. In case you missed this the first time, it's a good idea. Hospitals, which are not hotels, have to stick to a budget. After tearing through a whole pack of wipes in no time flat for her son's meconium blowouts, Chara was told to use a stack of wet brown paper towels from the bathroom. Seriously. It is, in fact, the reason for the largest argument in the history of Chara's marriage. Partners, take note: arguing with the woman who just delivered a baby is strategically dead-end. Hormones are more powerful than syllogism. Just sayin'.

- Bring petroleum jelly. Meconium is very hard to remove from baby's skin. Applying Vaseline around the bum makes a world of wiping difference.

- Don't be afraid to co-sleep with your infant (versus keeping baby in the bassinet as the nurse suggested for liability purposes), or give the baby a pacifier while in the hospital. Neither is habit forming in these first 48 hours of life, please! Understand there is a real physiological need for sucking and human connection. The pacifier may be the only way to keep the baby from crying without cracking your nipples and you need them in good working order for the long haul!

- Expect to be discharged fairly promptly based on your medical condition, not your emotional or practical readiness to pack up and return home. Again, the hospital isn't a hotel, which is why there's no "late check-out" option. Don't settle in too much.

Front door sign

Make a sign and tape it over the doorbell stating: "Do not ring doorbell – baby sleeping" or "Please knock gently" or "Go the fuck away" (thus saving unnecessary conversation). This is your chance to see what 96-pt Calibri bold looks like at a distance. Don't be concerned that you are the only nutty person with this kind of notice on your door. During her house remodel, second-time-mom Chara added a switch to disconnect the doorbell at nap-time. Hallelujah.

Baby bald spot is not cute (says Chara)

For the first three months, babies can't lift their heads, and as such their heads are always in contact with your arm, bed, blanket, back of an upholstered car seat or carrier. The friction creates a funny-looking bald strip on the back of his or her head. With her second child, Chara learned, that placing a tiny silk blanket behind his head (in carriers and cribs) keeps the hair on. Totally works – no bald spot! Or just take Helen's advice: don't sweat the small stuff.

Loveys

Many children become attached to a "lovey" – typically a silky blanket or a stuffed animal. Chara's first child lives for the lovey... and at age nine, she can't sleep without it. Helen's children also have loveys and continue to be attached to them despite major disintegration. To this day, Helen is kicking herself for not buying three identical loveys per child. Keep two in rotation to slow down the wear and tear (and over 10 years, that is a lot), and store one new as a replacement. If a lovey gets lost or left behind at the most inconvenient of times, you have a backup!

Administering eye drops

It is common for your infant/toddler to need eye drops: pink eye (conjunctivitis), impetigo, yes – this is your life. Naturally, the moment you try and administer the drop, the kid shuts their eyes. The older they get, the more WWF it becomes. The best practice is to lay the child down, let them shut their eyes, hold their head steady between your knees, and place the eye drop inside their eye well. When the kid opens their eyes, the medicine will slip right in (as long as their head remains steady and straight).

Chara's method: Expedite matters by handing the child a surprise gift or treat. The suspense will open their eyes that much sooner. Helen's method: Administer the eye drop, quickly say, "blink blink blink!" and hand the kids tissues for the excess. Let's move on, no treat.

Mattress pads galore – starting with the crib
Potty training up to age eight is part of your life, so this tip has non-trivial implications. The reality is hundreds of wet beds per child, requiring sheet-changing **in the middle of the night**. Fact: diapers and pull-ups leak, kids start to refuse them even when only partially night trained, and accidents continue to occur long after diapers are out of the equation. Just when you think you're safe, relatively big changes may translate into bedwetting, such as getting used to the longer, more structured kindergarten day, a new sibling, an inexperienced caregiver, or a parent going back to work. Therefore, invest and put on your registry a good quality, washable, high-absorbency, waterproof "bedwetting overlay." Although more expensive than a fitted waterproof mattress pad, it is much easier to use, more absorbent and lasts forever, vs. the mattress cover whose cheap plastic waterproofing starts to disintegrate with repeat machine washes (and you only figure this out after it starts to leak).

Bedwetting preparedness instructional
(for both bed and crib mattress):

- Start off with a plastic waterproof cover that zips entirely around the mattress.
- On top of that, place a fitted waterproof mattress pad.
- On top of that, place a sheet.
- On top of that, place a high-absorbency bed bedwetting mattress overlay. It's big, has good weight, lies flat, and covers the entire bed surface.
- On top of which your child sleeps.

When accidents occur, *voila,* you need only lift up the overlay. Helen figured out how to do this in her sleep, after (stupidly) trying to change all the sheets in the wee hours during potty training. Note: it also works well for sick kids who are vomiting or have diarrhea.

CPSIA information can be obtained
at www.ICGtesting.com
Printed in the USA
FSOW04n1935121015
12128FS